TICKET TO RIDE

A Rail Journey Around Australia

An early morning storm is brewing as the Gulflander *leaves Croydon Station.*

TICKET TO RIDE

A Rail Journey Around Australia

ANTHONY DENNIS AND
MICHAEL RAYNER

Prentice Hall Press

To all those who prefer to fly. May they be converted...

 Prentice Hall Press
15 Columbus Circle
New York, New York 10023

First published in Australasia in 1989 by
Simon & Schuster Australia
7 Grosvenor Place, Brookvale NSW 2100

Distributed in the United States by Prentice Hall Press,
a division of Simon & Schuster, Inc.

P‍rentice H‍all P‍ress and colophons are trademarks of
Simon & Schuster, Inc.

© Text Anthony Dennis 1989
Photographs Michael Rayner 1989

All rights reserved. No part of this publication may be reproduced,
stored in a retrieval system, or transmitted, in any form or
by any means, electronic, mechanical, photocopying, recording
or otherwise, without the prior permission of the publisher
in writing.

ISBN: 0-13-921198-5

Designed by Jack Jagtenberg
Map by Risetto Pty Limited
Typeset in Australia by Midland Typesetters Pty Ltd
Printed in Hong Kong by South China Printing Company

A child passenger looks out at Goondiwindi from the Dirranbandi Mail.
The Wroblewski family survey the scene at sunset at Redmont railway camp.

FOREWORD BY CLIVE ROBERTSON

I remember the first time I confronted a steam locomotive. I threw an aniseed ball at a 53 class goods loco from the overhead bridge at Lawson (just near the Literary Institute) in the Blue Mountains, due west of Sydney. I ran all the way home for fear of retribution. No one can possibly understand the nerve it took to do that. I was about five.

I hesitate now, in my 44th year, to wax anything about the railways, let alone a steam vehicle. You see, the business of train-locomotive-enjoying-riding has attracted an unfair share of the mental-fringe-dwellers, those *loonies* who inflict anyone in sight with the most useless information. That and their quarter-track, three-and-three-quarter-inches-per-second mono recordings, their 127 Kodak cameras, and an indefatigable urge to be in every seat on the train really do tend to put me off.

I did, however, work for the railways (some might see that as unique in itself). I've never told anyone this, but I joined up because of steam. The part of my brain that perceives the demise of the joyful saw steam disappearing amongst the smog. I remember those halcyon days of real-life fantasy, driving a large V-class in the wheat belt of Western Australia. What made the dream quite real was that particular day when it was 156°F in the cab of the locomotive. One pays for one's fantasies.

Train travel, of course, however powered, is for the child in oneself. Gazing out the window while listening to the irregular noises of conflicting metals can trigger the mind. Or am I talking about the heart? For me, at least, it's the solitude. Just the locomotive and me. Why is a train so wonderful? Why is this large, noisy, illogical thing on parallel rail so consistently alluring? Why, apart from the full-pipe church organ, is the steam locomotive man's greatest achievement? And, more important, why did we so willingly leave it behind? What is it that happens to the lone traveller on a train and nowhere else?

It was with these mixed emotions, and a desire for adventure, that young Mr Dennis and his friend Mr Rayner ventured forth to try to capture something of the perennial joys of rail. On reflection, it's a jolly pity they didn't ask me to come along. I've got this marvellous new camera, an equally wonderful, cute little tape recorder, and all those really tremendous tapes at home . . . Oh well, at least I've got the book . . . and a heart.

ACKNOWLEDGMENTS

Many people shook their heads in bewilderment when we suggested the idea of a book about train travel in Australia. A few of them, we think, are still confounded that we made such a journey. But aren't the best journeys of all those which leave people incredulous? It was, of course, no joy-ride. Before we left Central Station we spent many, many hours locked away with Lloyd Smith of the New South Wales State Rail Authority, Travel and Tours office, at Wynyard. Without his patience and sense of humour to see the absurdity of such a trip, we would have been left standing where we started. He plotted our route, booked our tickets, and shared the adventure even though he remained comparatively stationary.

We would like to thank the *Sydney Morning Herald* for its financial support of the trip and for its publication of a series of articles on which *Ticket To Ride* is loosely based. The photographic editor of the *Herald*, Julian Zakaris, was a singularly great supporter of the project and we thank him too.

The cameras would have been empty of film much sooner if it were not for the generous support of Mark Lee from the Professional Photography Division at Kodak Australia. It was Kodak who supplied the hundreds of rolls of Kodachrome colour and black and white film for the journey.

The publisher of Simon & Schuster, Kirsty Melville, entertained our modest scheme to catch every train we could squeeze into a month and a half with an enthusiasm and reassurance that we valued when we wished we were home. It was Kirsty, above everyone else, who understood what we were on about.

We would like to thank Alan Ward and his staff at Vision Graphics, Sydney, for the tireless processing and labelling of literally thousands of transparencies from our exploits.

The back-packs, rain-jackets and walking shoes we wore on the journey, which withstood terrible punishment, were supplied by the adventure travel suppliers Kathmandu, Sydney and Melbourne.

The lift we received from Jamie Cooper of the Gulf Transport Co Pty Ltd from Wyndham to Fitzroy Crossing was greatly appreciated.

Our time at the Mount Newman Mining camp, Redmont, was enjoyable, but the uncommon goodwill of David O'Neill (who has since left the Mount Newman camp) made it memorable.

The co-operation of Australian National and Westrail was invaluable.

And, perhaps most of all, we should express our profound gratitude for the Australians and, indeed, those foreigners who travelled on Australia's trains. You stopped, chatted and were candid on cue. You stood still and smiled when the camera clicked. And because we liked you all, we'll tell you a secret. It wasn't really the trains we wanted to meet—it was you who rode them...

Anthony Dennis and Michael Rayner, March 1989

CONTENTS

FOREWORD   5
ACKNOWLEDGMENTS   6
MAP   8
1   THE PACIFIC COAST MOTORAIL   11
2   THE DIRRANBANDI MAIL   20
3   THE WESTLANDER AND THE MIDLANDER   35
4   THE QUEENSLANDER   46
5   THE GULFLANDER   57
6   THE IRON ORE TRAIN   70
7   THE INDIAN PACIFIC   85
8   THE TEA AND SUGAR   98
9   THE GHAN   113
10   THE BLUE LAKE, THE INTER-CITY DAYLINK, THE SUNRAYSIA, THE SILVER CITY COMET AND THE XPT   124
APPENDIX
RAIL INFORMATION   141
APPENDIX
PHOTOGRAPHIC INFORMATION   143
INDEX   144

The beginning of the journey—a frenetic Boxing Day at Sydney's Central Station, 6.15 pm.

CHAPTER ONE
THE PACIFIC COAST MOTORAIL

It was bedlam at Sydney's Central Station that steamy, stormy Boxing Day afternoon when we arrived to catch a train. Inside the luggage office an impromptu cabaret, starring a Mussolini in blue railway shorts, was occurring. From behind his scales the tyrant barked his by-laws at the sodden passengers, their composure brittle even before they had boarded a train. The rain thumped on the immense vaulted roof, all iron and glass, like a tone-deaf calypso band as the passengers were scolded by Mussolini for their ignorance of the railway by-laws. A limp procession of bodies, shirts pasted to flesh from the heat and the wet, dragged their chattels from one end of the station to the other, dodging the pond made by a drip from the ceiling. I found a dry seat and fanned myself with our thick wad of damp tickets.

A railway station is, of course, the most unfashionable of places to be for the modern long-distance traveller. A train takes so *long*. But any rail-fancier realises that time is hardly the point. Before the screech of the jet-engine blasted rail forever from our lives, the platform was the only place for the serious itinerant. The art of train travel is doomed. One day soon, except for a bland collection of tourist and museum trains delicately and lovingly restored, the train in Australia will balance on the brink of extinction. All over the country venerable old lines, relics of a languid era long gone, have been erased from maps. Everywhere buses, in clouds of choking fumes, traverse the tracks of their fallen forebears, despatching their sullen prisoners from one comfort stop to the next. Before it was too late—before the auditors' sharpened pencils could decree that another line be closed—we left Sydney and its urban neuroses in search of lost times. It would be a railway safari in search of a dying species, armed only with the modest intention of riding every train that rolled into our sights in a month and a half. Where there were no trains we would travel by any mode of transport presenting itself along our 20,000 km route from Central Station to Central Station—an epic loop, the distance between Sydney and London. A rag-tag collection of trains lay ahead, all listed on the tickets. Among them was the *Queenslander* to the far tropics;

the *Gulflander* through the Gulf of Carpentaria; the giant *Mount Newman Mining* train between Port Hedland and Newman; the *Indian Pacific* and the *Tea and Sugar* across the Nullarbor; the *Ghan* to the Red Centre; and the *Silver City Comet* from Broken Hill.

It was raining harder at Central Station now and the roof was taking a fearful battering. For that matter, so were those unfortunates who filed through the luggage room. The foul mood of the blue-shorts Mussolini now matched the weather outside.

"Hey you, queue here!" he screamed. He might have been merely shouting to be heard above the din on the roof, but I suspected this was a regular performance. "No, no, no, no!" he yelled, arms wild as a malfunctioning windmill. "Sign here! Hey you! Don't do that again! Your bag! Why hasn't it got a name on it? Please, please, put your name on it!"

On a railway system burdened with a debt heinous enough to inspire a coup in a third world country, the staff had apparently abandoned courtesies long ago. Despite it all, I enjoyed Mussolini's antics immensely, though it was clear none of my fellow passengers in that damp luggage room shared my sense of theatre. One of Mussolini's victims, drenched from the storm, muttered obscenities as he tied a Murwillumbah tag to the handle of his suitcase. "Bloody maniac!" the man muttered. He was stunned when Mussolini, a man clearly imbued with a sadistic sense of humour, grinned and wished him a Happy New Year.

Play abandoned due to rain, as a youngster waits for the delayed Pacific Coast Motorail *at Central Station.*

The railway platform, perhaps quite like nowhere else, remains forever the home of the long farewell.

A collection of rubber stamps, one for every destination, hung from a white board, a salient reflection of the antiquated railway system which paid Mussolini's wages. The anachronistic rubber stamps offered proof that the railways had stalled in the 1960s, remained locked in another era and emerged when it was too late. The *Pacific Coast Motorail*, the train that would launch us on the journey, rolled into the platform just as Mussolini was humiliating a Dubbo-bound woman. I decided it was time for intermission.

I would have liked to write that I have had a lengthy love affair with rail. It is almost compulsory for the chronicler of trains to make such a confession but for me, that would have been a lie. There are those who speak longingly of the bewitchment trains cast on them in childhood, when a loco would scream past their bedroom window and they longed to be on it. I would hide in my pillowcase until it had gone. It was not until later in life when I caught the *International Express* from Bangkok to Singapore that I realised the potential of rail. I still recall the Buddhist monk in full regalia but with a digital watch and designer suitcase, with whom I shared my compartment. I also remember the Iranian who was fleeing from the Ayatollah and wanted to buy my Australian jeans. On a train you meet an odd assortment of humans

with such an array of reasons for travelling, all jumbled together and forced to communicate. On a train you can escape from objectionable company; on a bus there is nowhere to hide, but there is the lounge car, the dining car and your cabin on the train. And on a jet only a sedative can rescue you from becoming a Siamese twin of the stranger in the next seat. It is only on a train that you do not get sea-sick, air-sick or car-sick.

Yet I admit that on board the *Pacific Coast Motorail* to Murwillumbah, via Casino, with the rain dribbling off the roof, I *was* overcome with an attack of rail-sickness—and the train was still stationary on the platform! I suspect it was the whispered conversation I overheard from the seat in front of me in the economy carriage that did it.

"Hey, let's have a party!" said one of a quartet of teenagers—three girls and a boy—as the others compiled an inventory of the alcohol they had smuggled aboard the train. "I've got a bottle of vodka . . . Hey, I wonder where the bar is on this train?" another asked. "No, wait till the train starts moving," said another. "It's more fun then."

It was serious enough that the train was already half an hour late, but the conversation foreshadowed the long night ahead. Young minds think alike and if those teenagers, determined to defy their bodily calendar and thrust themselves into adulthood, were planning a party, I surmised that so too would all their contemporaries slowly filling the train and toting innocent-looking soft-drink bottles laced with illicit booze. It was *verboten* to bring alcohol aboard the train, of course, though the methods of concealment practised by the young passengers of the *Pacific Coast Motorail* would have been admired at Colditz.

It was raining so heavily now that those on the platform farewelling their loved ones through the windows were forced to retreat from the edge of the platform for cover. A railway guard on a yellow buggy wove his way between the overstacked baggage trolleys scattered near the brake van. The father of one of the conspiratorial teenagers squashed his face against the window of the carriage for a last goodbye as one of them struggled violently to conceal their cache. The train slowly pulled away from the platform. The teenagers sighed the sigh of all teenagers relieved of parental control and poured themselves a celebratory drink.

It was dark now and the rain sprayed the foggy windows. The humidity had gone, for now we were encased in an air-conditioned cocoon as the north-bound *Motorail* ignored the scruffy suburban stations—molested by vandalism and graffiti—and gradually shed the city precincts until there was nothing to see outside except intermittent lights and illuminated droplets.

Already it was clear, I had decided, that by the next morning the *Pacific Coast Motorail* would become the Hangover Express, a vomitorium on wheels. An hour later the remnants of the banana fritter sundaes in the dining car were sloshing seductively back and forth in melted ice-cream to the rhythm of the train. The second sitting was announced over the public address by a waitress with a sinus problem as the first-sitting diners were about to be dismissed.

The special-of-the-day was an intriguingly coloured veal casserole but Susan, the telephonist with a full-blown case of linguistic dysentery, ordered a salad and a bottle of "trem-een-er reezling". The waiter's eyebrows elevated alarmingly and he sniffed at her pronunciation. His reaction was a trifle presumptuous since the dining car of the *Pacific Coast Motorail* was most definitely not the Ritz.

"I assume that will be a bottle of the tram-in-er riesling, madam?" Susan might have been offended but she was a woman on a mission with no time for pedants. She had taken the *Pacific Coast Motorail* to rescue her girlfriend who had mistakenly returned to the dangerous embrace of her former husband.

"It's a real mess," she sighed, pricking the lettuce with her fork and thereby squirting salad dressing into my casserole. "The problem is that he's absolutely gorgeous, a real spunk, and she's gorgeous too. They just can't keep their hands off each other. She can't resist him—even though he bashes her up. That's why she left him in the first place. It's funny, you know. I reckon at least three-quarters of my girlfriends get bashed up by their husbands. One of them says she'll turn gay in a few years. She reckons, at any rate, it'd be safer."

It was a harrowing conversation for so early on the trip. There were, after all, 19,734 km still in front of us. By now our seductive banana fritters had arrived and Susan had forgotten her girlfriend's woes. She enjoyed her job answering telephones at International Directory Assistance: "Sometimes it's like taking an overseas trip without the jet-lag." Her favourite number to dial was the one that summoned the Australian Antarctic bases by radio telephone, because she got to say "roger" and "over". At the other end of the line, however, were hidden terrors.

"The Saudi Arabians are the worst, you know," she said. "When we ring them for a number they tell us to get the men operators to call them back because the bastards refuse point blank to speak to a woman operator. They're such bloody chauvinists. But we fix 'em. We get the gay operators to call them, don't we? Not much bloody difference, eh?"

It was still raining heavily outside and it was wet inside, too. After dessert was digested it became clear that several of the passengers were already

Night-time on the Pacific Coast Motorail *and the battle for slumber begins.*

A boy peers from his economy class window on the north-bound Motorail.

Top *The* Brisbane Limited—*our connection between Casino and Brisbane—leaves Lismore Station in a gentle drizzle.* **Above** *A smoker, relegated to the vestibule for a puff, contemplates the lush hinterland of Queensland's south-east corner on the* Brisbane Limited *from Casino.*

drunk. A no-go area had already been declared by the tee-total passengers—the smoking carriage next door, which had come to resemble a sordid snooker room without the table but with much of the vice. There in the smog a fearful contingent of boozed, rowdy young men were immersed in pornographic magazines, the nude centrefolds of which they had pinned to the walls and luggage racks of the carriage. A female passenger cringed and fell asleep. A few seats away was a bald, bearded, middle-aged man who had smuggled aboard a jumbo-sized bottle of soft drink laced liberally with bourbon. He struggled, in a doped state, over the strewn limbs in the aisle in yet another bilious sprint to the toilet. In the darkened vestibule a hippy bound for Nimbin was crouched, cigarette in mouth, breast-feeding her baby.

Towards midnight the lights in the carriage were extinguished and the battle for slumber began. A procession of drunks staggered through the carriage on their way back to the animal car. The burly man across the aisle had appointed himself night-watchman. He drifted in and out of sleep and sprinkled his waking moments with graphic threats of violence against the noise-makers at the other end of the carriage. A young teenage boy with a severe haircut was taking snap-shots with a blinding flash which, for a split second, drenched the carriage in a fleeting white light. The night-watchman, infuriated, squeezed past his sleeping female companion and marched down the aisle. If the camera flashed again, he warned, it would become an instamatic suppository. Despite the threat, a raucous party continued in the vestibule and did not stop until the last drop of contraband and legal booze was consumed.

Beside me was Barry, an ex-truckie who had lost two discs from his back in an operation after a refrigerator had fallen on him. He was wounded when I complained that he was a loud snorer. "Yeah, well, you would be too if you had to take all the medication I'm under," he said. Barry was biding his time till the compo cheque arrived bearing the six-figure sum. Just when the night-watchman grabbed an intoxicated 16-year-old by his blonde locks, I fell asleep on Barry's bad back.

The next morning the first call for breakfast—"Please bring your reservation tickets to secure a table"—was announced at 6.30 am. I expected the night-watchman to wake up fighting, but he was sleeping like a sedated infant. The revellers of the night before moaned in agony as the first rays of sun squeezed under the shutters. The smoking car, the scene of widespread debauchery the night before, now resembled the scene of a fatal derailment.

The uneventful three hours we then spent on the *Brisbane Limited* from Casino to Brisbane provided a good chance for us to recuperate from the *Motorail* trip.

CHAPTER TWO
THE DIRRANBANDI MAIL

It was dusk at Brisbane's Roma Street Station when the guard's whistle shrilled and the *Dirranbandi Mail*, like an untethered museum exhibit, rattled away from the platform bound for all stations to nowhere in particular. The train looked frail enough for the slipstream of any sudden movement to peel the flaky paint off the old wooden passenger carriages, miraculous survivors of the rolling stock graveyard. The guards had guided us aboard in a fit of urgency, jamming our suitcases into the vestibule of the carriage until we were off—along one of the most plodding railway routes in Australia. Once on the train there could be but one certainty: the *Dirranbandi Mail* could never suffer the perils of over-booking. Our only companions in the first-class carriage were an Aboriginal family and a rabid rail-buff.

Despite its age, the interior of the sleeping carriage, in contrast to its exterior, seemed to have remained in pristine condition. It was resplendent in finely preserved wood-panelling, varnished until you could see your reflection, and its rich green leather upholstery had somehow escaped the vandal's knife. A shiny silver toilet bowl popped out of the wall, big enough for any size bum. There was no air-conditioning and it was suffocating inside the berth. I switched on an antique fan attached to the wall near the ceiling and it buzzed back at me like a berserk blowfly.

Every time it leaves Roma Street Station the *Dirranbandi Mail* is loaded with untold tonnages of nostalgia, though it is kept almost a secret by Queensland Railways, perhaps for fear of ridicule. It is primarily a freight train that sheds its carriages as it nears the end of the line. Queensland Railways, as a gesture of goodwill, attaches a couple of passenger carriages to the *Dirranbandi Mail* for its journey to the boundary of the never-never and back again. The *Mail* is a whimsical anachronism on bogeys. Almost all the old long-distance trains with sleeping berths without air-conditioning have been withdrawn from service. Yet the *Mail* seems to survive on some weary sense of purpose. It would have been convenient—and perhaps saner—for us to have taken the simpler route to Cairns, straight up the coastline on the luxurious *Queenslander*. We could have been there in a day. But we were headed west

The Dirranbandi Mail, *like an untethered museum piece, emerges from a tunnel beneath the prosperous Brisbane skyline.*

in search of a forgotten era and the tropics could wait. Besides, *true* adventure is seldom found in a padded armchair at break-neck speeds.

An hour or so out of Brisbane the Taylor family, all six of them, were squeezed into a couple of economy sleeping berths with three tiers of beds. The lofty top bunk was so high off the floor that Queensland railways might have been advised to insist on abseiling experience for those courageous souls who chose to sleep up there. The father, Bruce, was a fettler based at Dirranbandi, a town dependent on its once-a-week train. His wife Keitha—her parents had wanted a boy—worked a few days a week at the local betting agency. A week later on the trip they were still producing the murky family snapshot taken en route to Brisbane when the *Mail* derailed after a cargo container tumbled off a carriage. The couple's 10-year-old son Jason had toppled from the top bunk onto the floor from the impact of the crunching carriages. The Taylors were delayed an eternity—a long time even on the *Dirranbandi Mail*.

High-rise living on the Mail. *The Taylor family, Jason (top) Kira (middle) and father, Bruce, languish in their compartment as the hot breeze off the plains heats up the carriage.*

It became cooler and darker as the *Mail* sneaked through mountain terraces near Toowoomba dotted with tiny wooden stations lit by a single light bulb, and dodged the inclines that had already stalled our progress. The thick, tall eucalyptus trees on either side of the track were bathed in the locomotive's arc of yellow light. At first, I sat on the running board with the door wide open, but I was forced inside for warmth. After the steaminess we had left behind in Brisbane, it was difficult for a southerner like me to conceive that it could be so chilly in the midst of a Queensland summer. I wandered through the dim passageway of the carriage in search of company and found a middle-aged man in the next compartment wiggling his bare toes. He introduced himself as Charles Reich and it appeared that he did not wish to be disturbed. But I interrupted his solitude for I needed to forge a bond for the expedition. There were few enough of us as it was for the endurance test ahead. We were in this one together. I poked my head into the darkness and asked jokingly where I could locate the dining car.

"Oh, there's no dining car on this train, I'm afraid," he said earnestly. He had removed his beige walk-socks and hung them neatly on a couple of hooks on the wall. His radio, tuned permanently to the ABC, was balanced on the window's edge and there was steaming hot coffee in his big blue vacuum flask. Here was a picture of contented regimentation. His abrupt manner, however, suggested that he was a school-master and, sure enough, he explained that he was a principal at a Cairns high school and, moreover, a passionate rail-buff with an avid interest in rolling stock, and a scoutmaster who had officiated at a World Scout Jamboree. He sat quietly in the darkness, occasionally switching on the reading light above his head to study the

Ever-vigilant for "mile-pegs", "line-switches" and the intricacies of the "working timetable", rail-buff, school principal and scout-leader, Charles Reich, emerges from his teak-panelled compartment on the Dirranbandi Mail.

Top *The sole recipient of a dining service on the* Mail *was a whimpering, though well-nourished canine, the resident of a box in the brake van.*   **Above** *The undulations to the east dissolve, as the* Mail *travels across parched plains, skirting the Queensland and New South Wales borders. For some the relentless journey is tedium, but for Kira and Jason Taylor, there is adventure down the line.*

"working timetable" which offered intricate details of the *Mail*'s passage to Dirranbandi. For him, the long trip was obviously an enjoyable experience.

At Toowoomba Station the *Mail* stopped for half an hour to load and unload freight. A couple of railway workers boarded the train and claimed the vacant sleeping berths, locked their doors and went to sleep. The jewel of the station was a marvellous old dining-room which appeared to have remained unaltered since the 1930s. It was late by then and the lights had long been extinguished in the lovely dining-room and its kitchen, whose stoves had probably served nothing more exotic than roast lamb with mint sauce. There was a bar with ornate wooden tables and chairs and not a soul in sight. The deserted dining-room was melancholy. It would never again witness the surge of customers it welcomed in its glorious past. It was remarkable enough that it was still there at all. Yet the dining-room had been preserved perhaps not just from devotion, but possibly due to that indefatigable strain of conservatism that characterises Queensland Railways and the state itself. Not unlike the *Dirranbandi Mail*, it stood as a working museum to a once fashionable era of railway travel. On the walls hung dusty pictures dating back to the days of steam and portraits of those who toiled on a once busy line. Standing in that dining-room it was impossible not to bemoan the demise of the venerable age of Australian railway travel when dozens of trains steamed through Toowoomba on their way to the outback, which in those days would have been truly remote. Many Queensland country railway stations would have once had dining-rooms as grand as this one, but Toowoomba was one of the few to maintain its link with the past. A neon light flickered, the bar opened, and in came Bruce Taylor and the boy in the fedora who had asked me on the Roma Street platform if I was the new teacher destined for the Dirranbandi schoolyard. They each hurriedly drank a can of beer during the half-hour stop.

The antiquity of the first class cabin on the Dirranbandi Mail *shows in a highly polished basin.*

The only food aboard the *Mail* was the tin of Chum pet food the guards had ordered for the whimpering, boxed canine in the brake van. Here, and down the line, the only sustenance came during forays to the general stores in towns beside the track. The station kiosk served microwaved sausage rolls and stolid meat pies, sold by an exasperated middle-aged woman who complained of the noise from the refrigerated freight carriage opposite.

On the platform, Mr Reich, wearing a pair of thongs, said that he planned to ride the *Mail* to Dirranbandi. There he would sleep for a few hours in the hot afternoon, in an air-conditioned room at the local pub. He would rise, partially rejuvenated, to take the train all the way back again to Brisbane. By the time he staggered onto the Roma Street platform he would be either a broken man or a hero. It would be a feat intrepid enough to rival the purchase of a return ticket on the *Trans-Siberian Express*. But he was a rail-buff and

At Roma Street Station, a suburban commuter, groceries in hand, looks distainfully, as Queensland Railway's classified secret, the Dirranbandi Mail, *edges away from the platform.*

TICKET TO RIDE

obsession is a potent propellent. At Roma Street, where a jungle of tropical flora billowed with palms and ferns, Mr Reich had arrived with his itinerary prepared with the coolest precision. In his teaching days, before he was appointed principal, he had taught mathematics and German, and the benefits of both subjects were palpable. He had painstakingly prepared the exact distances between each stop, and the times of arrivals and departures. He was a marvel who, once you understood his motivation, commanded a profound admiration, if not a feeling of warmth.

At Roma Street the day before, the clerk at the ticket window giggled when I showed him our tickets to Dirranbandi. "Why in God's name would you want to go to Dirranbandi?" he asked with a smirk and a hint of sadism. He was the last Queensland Railways employee to scrutinise our tickets. It was almost as though, sympathetic to the plight of those forced to endure the *Mail*, they didn't wish to make the trip any more arduous by demanding to see a ticket. They had asked enough of us to *pay* to ride the rambling antique in the first place. I unhinged the bed, with its crisp white railway linen, from its resting-place in the wall of my berth and drifted off to sleep. The swirling breeze that squeezed through the slightly open slats of the shuttered window gently massaged my face and I felt contented as the train bounced down the line like a cargo-laden trampoline.

By road, the journey to Dirranbandi—600 km west of Brisbane on the distant side of the Great Dividing Range—takes a comparatively swift seven hours. On the train to Dirran', as the locals call it, the ride consumes almost a full day's travel. Despite its nightmarish qualities, this is one of the great undiscovered Australian railway journeys. It is certainly a frugal experience. All you really need before you leave Roma Street is an injection of patience.

Everywhere down the line it was rumoured that the service would be closed. The auditors, disturbed by the *Mail*'s losses, would probably prefer to watch it be derailed forever by official decree. But the *Mail* is a twice-weekly lifeline for the minuscule townships along one of the country's most obscure railway routes. What is more, the piercing whistle-blast of the approaching train symbolises a restoration of morale and a confirmation that jobs are safe.

When I woke the next morning the coolness had been replaced by a sticky, hot breeze. Outside, the undulations had vanished. The terrain had been sapped of moisture and flattened by Nature's rolling-pin in the night. A shaven and scented Mr Reich emerged from his berth and announced, in a voice you would expect at school assembly, that he had slept longer "than initially anticipated". There was a sense of cheerful intimacy between nature

At Thallon, near Dirranbandi, after almost a day out of Brisbane, a wise-cracking station-master and an impish local, farewell the departing Mail. *In a few hours it will be back again for the return journey east.*

Top *The only relief from the heat and the boredom of an interminable journey at last near its end: a bottle of warm, though welcome beer and the first, distant glimpse of home at Dirranbandi.* **Above** *The end of the line if there ever was one. The track to Dirranbandi goes no further, but on the brink of the never never the desolate western plains of Queensland seem to extend forever.*

and passenger on the *Dirranbandi Mail.* Here you could poke your head out of the window and sniff the breeze; listen to the wheels skidding sharply over the steel tracks; chat to a fellow passenger in the economy carriage without getting out of your seat, just by poking your head out of a window. The guard was ensconced in the brake van so I opened the door, sat on the edge and dangled my feet outside as the crisp paspalum beside the track thrashed the soles of my shoes and the wind blow-waved my hair.

The train lurched to a halt at Goondiwindi Railway Station. All the shops along the line, just like the kiosk back at Toowoomba, had offered facsimile menus: sausage rolls or meat pies microwaved beyond consumption. Each was staffed, confoundingly, by the same full-hipped Queensland wife wearing a floral summer dress and a sullen demeanour. There was plenty of time for meat pies and sausage rolls. The *Dirranbandi Mail* stops, for wildly varying periods, on at least two dozen occasions. I knew that because Mr Reich was kind enough to write them all down for me on a page from his notebook. For breakfast the Goondiwindi kiosk had only toast and Vegemite wrapped in foil, and hot coffee. On the platform I found a seat, unwrapped my toast with the vigour of a famine victim, and sipped my coffee. I suspected we would be re-entering the meat pie and sausage roll zone with half a day left to travel. I noticed that Mr Reich had wandered into the station-master's office with his coffee to inspect the old-fashioned ticket-dispenser and exchange unintelligible railway jargon with the guard. I had slowly warmed to Mr Reich. When I merely asked him his estimation of the age of our carriage he sacrificed his dash across the lines for a meat pie or sausage roll, and devoted the entire stop to searching the carriage for the plate that would indicate its date of commission. Anyone with such a boundless love for anything must be imbued with some depth of goodness.

For such an epic trip the dénouement is less than dramatic. The last stop was a dusty outback town with a pub and a twice-a-week train. If there was ever an end of the line, Dirranbandi—which they say was a one-horse town before the nag died of heat exhaustion—was it. Almost a full day later, the *Mail* lurched into the station. I recalled what its laconic engineman, Ken McPherson, had told me in the cabin as we trundled down the track with just a few carriages behind us: "We're in no hurry out here."

Although I appreciated Ken's observation, Dirranbandi, a day after Roma Street, was a long way to go to hear such a bold understatement. There was the usual Dirranbandi welcoming party to greet the train. Once the train stopped, Mr Reich gingerly leapt off. With his big blue flask tucked under his right arm, his radio silent inside his gladstone bag, the notebook safely in his pocket, and an ironed shirt on a hanger over his shoulder, Mr Reich trod the trail to the hotel.

CHAPTER THREE
THE WESTLANDER AND THE MIDLANDER

The kangaroo shooter's battered utility bounded down the unsealed track, cratered with pot-holes, like the hopping national symbol that it stalked at night. It was so hot on that dusty road to Cunnamulla that the blowflies had started to drink the insect repellent as an aperitif. The air-conditioner wheezed, spluttered, coughed and died. For a moment we were off the rails headed for the next connection. At the end of the line we had exchanged the narrow gauge for the open road: dirt here, bitumen there. All the way from Brisbane, now a day away, the *Dirranbandi Mail* had dispatched us to the outpost from which the train derived its name. It was the sort of town that gives the term "the middle of nowhere" its bad reputation. Earlier at the railway station, as we disembowelled the carriage of our suitcases and assorted cargo, an Aboriginal boy on the platform looked at me with the kind of smirk reserved for all interlopers.

"Hey mate!" he called. "Welcome to the land of the never-never." Not far away, a man in a blue singlet waited to take us on a sort of guided tour of this mythical place. At the service station where Barry Cocks, the kangaroo shooter, stopped to refuel the utility for the three-hour drive ahead, a trio of men were doing the same for their four-wheel drive. They were obviously not friendly locals.

"And don't call me a c . . ., right?" the T-shirted one snarled at Michael, our photographer, who mistakenly thought they were joking.

"Sorry?" he said.

"Don't call me a c . . ., I said." It was the first antagonism we had struck since we left Sydney, apart from the man on the *Pacific Coast Motorail* who

At Kubill siding, on the line between Cunnamulla and Charleville, the Westlander *stops briefly to deliver mail to a local grazier who has driven from his homestead to meet the train.*

(35)

threatened to turn the kid's camera into a suppository. The annoyance of the man in the T-shirt was a mystery, for Michael had merely said hello. If one of our limbs was to be broken it would be better for the sake of the book, we decided, if it happened in more spectacular circumstances than a brawl, so we fled with not so much as a rude gesture out the back window.

It was, sure enough, an odd route to choose to get to Cairns. The deserted road between Dirranbandi and Cunnamulla, a three-hour drive dodging frenzied sheep and corrugations, would convey us to the next train, the *Westlander* to Charleville. From there we would catch a bus to Longreach to rendezvous with the *Midlander* to Rockhampton where we would wait for the *Queenslander* to Cairns. By the time we arrived, we would have pierced the heart of the state and exchanged thirsty scrub for lush tropics on an epic, though detoured, segment of the journey.

Back on the road with ridges thudding beneath us, Cocks warned us that we were in wild country. The night before, the local policeman had received a telephone call from a station owner who complained that illegal shooters had been firing on wild boars near to his homestead. A posse of sorts was formed among the local Dirranbandi citizens, and the pair was arrested. The feral bacon they had shot was confiscated and destroyed.

"Everyone's pretty nervous about these illegal shooters these days," Cocks said. "A couple of weeks ago a station owner told a couple of them to ping off when they were shooting too close to his homestead. The next thing he knew he was on the ground and they were kicking the hell out of him. They left him beside the road unconscious. He was in hospital for a couple of weeks recovering. They really did him over, that's for sure."

The stench of dead roo pervaded the cockpit of the vehicle—a mobile sauna in the heat—as we hurtled towards Cunnamulla. The countryside was as flat as a bare tabletop. On a lucky night Cocks, an ex-paint salesman who had swapped a spray gun for a marksman's rifle, brought a couple of thousand kilograms of roo meat back to town before dawn. It would become dinner for urban canine gullets. When the kangaroos did dodge his bullets by hiding desperately in the shadows, Cocks could still earn $400 in one shift. But on that night, the roos were reprieved—Cocks was too busy transporting a couple of train-hoppers. The road, by now, had left the bulldust behind and reverted to bitumen. We were on the outskirts of Cunnamulla. The domed roof of the railway station, built with corrugated iron over the tracks, appeared up ahead. Once the railway disappears, the townsfolk could transform the station into a gymnasium, although lodging our luggage with the stationmaster in the tortuous heat of the late afternoon was calisthenics enough.

After a drink in the pub across the road, the big brass bell was swung

Top *Barry Cocks, ex-paint salesman turned 'roo shooter, in the cabin of his four-wheel drive on the road to Cunnamulla.*   **Above** *On the* Westlander *line between Cunnamulla and Charleville, a trio of startled sheep dodge the dangerous trajectory of the train.*

Not a reveller in sight at sunset at Longreach Station on a lonely New Year's Eve, awaiting the arrival of the Midlander *from Winton to the west.*

gingerly by the guard on the platform. A clank or two and we were off as the *Westlander*, the daily passenger service on the loop to Brisbane, rolled away from the station. It was a relief to be back on the tracks again, but it was decidedly claustrophobic after the *Dirranbandi Mail*, where you could open the windows or dangle your feet on the running board without fear of admonishment. The doors on the *Westlander* were bolted and the conductor eyed potential troublemakers. An irritable old woman in the front row of the carriage hissed as we climbed aboard.

"I hope you realise this is a non-smoking carriage." It was the first and last we heard from her. She buried herself beneath a multi-coloured crocheted shawl, just like the type that appears weekly in women's magazines, to retain some warmth in the chilly climate on the train northbound for Charleville, five hours away. Elsewhere, the cook in the dining car was ready for the subdued night ahead. On the table in front of her were six full photograph albums—memories of several visits to Expo in Brisbane. Her family had taken hundreds of snapshots. Ever since the closing ceremony rendered her season pass useless, she has suffered withdrawal symptoms. All she had left were her memories and an impressive pictorial record—six bulging albums of instamatic memories. "I miss it, I really do. You know, I cried and cried when it was over. I really did."

One of the hidden dangers of train travel is that it plunges you into the company of the sort of people you spend an entire lifetime avoiding. It became distressingly obvious, as the *Westlander* dawdled through the night at the regulation 60 km an hour, that we were in the company of the most extraordinary drunkard. It was back at the railway hotel at Cunnamulla that I first noticed him; a man in his late 50s with the same sort of corrugations in his face we encountered on the road we took to get there. Somewhere at the railway hotel he must have left behind several thousand brain cells in a monstrous binge. I had watched him devour the staple foodstuff of the outback, a meat pie bathed in tomato sauce, but the dripping gravy acted like lava and left him in the most sordid state. His shirt—a plain blue one at the beginning of the journey—was now patterned with rivulets of gravy and chunks of meat. A few hours later, still not sober, his war with convenience food had launched its second offensive. He ordered a hamburger from the girl in the buffet car, in the kind of voice so many drunks use to disguise their insobriety—but the hamburger fought back. He staggered back to his seat, a defeated man, his co-ordination poisoned by the grog. From the collar of his shirt to the cuff of his trousers, he resembled a crumpled tablecloth that had been involved in a vicious food fight to the death. By the time we arrived at Charleville I found him prostrate in the corridor and was forced to step over him. Wrapped in a giant railway quilt, he was attempting to light a cigarette

Top *Half-way between Cunnamulla and Charleville, night drapes a cool canopy over the Westlander.* **Above** *In the thirsty back-blocks of western Queensland, windscreen wipers on buses are more often used to remove squashed bugs than droplets of rain.* **Right** *Longreach Railway Station, built in 1916, is a jewel of the Queensland Railway.*

and his upper lip still bore a slash of tomato sauce like a bad shaving nick. My parting thought was to leave the train immediately. The highly-volatile combination of the quilt, the flammable alcohol on his breath, and the naked flame of the gas-lighter would, I was sure, be enough to transform the carriage into charcoal in a matter of minutes.

It was New Year's Eve, but you might not have noticed. The *Midlander* from Longreach to Rockhampton was like a morgue. Before dawn that day, we had caught a Greyhound bus from Charleville—there are no trains to Longreach from there. The *Midlander*, a facsimile of the *Westlander*, left Longreach, home of Qantas, the Stockman's Hall of Fame and, it must be noted, not much else, at 8 pm. It was a terrible disappointment for we had boarded with visions of wild parties on a slow-moving train, with amiable company and unlimited champagne. Maybe even a few party hats, streamers and some novelty like a kazoo to add to the cheer. The only revelry within coo-ee of us, however, occurred at the packed and gaily-lit assembly halls beside the railway line. From town to town we caught glimpses of somebody else's fun behind the open doors of the halls. At the stops, we caught fragments of their laughter. But we were trapped inside a frigid canister on New Year's Eve with the water fountain in the first-class carriage vestibule as the only lubricant. I used my finger to make bubbles in the water in the cup, but it still didn't look like champagne. By 10 pm the few passengers on the train were all precariously near slumber. Even the elderly Englishmen in the economy carriage had abandoned their bridge game because of poor light and wearily—though gleefully—discussed Australia's parlous cricket fortunes.

The train edged perilously near midnight—and another year. The loneliness of the long-distance train-driver was accentuated even more that night. The *Midlander*'s engineman, Lloyd Vagg, and the fireman beside him, Jeff Clews, were like us—two travellers on a soul-destroying vigil. There was no champagne in the locomotive, just a billy to boil some weak tea, and only the dim illumination of the train's headlight. The atmosphere was melancholy. We had boarded the *Midlander* at Longreach expecting riotous revelry, but instead found ourselves aboard a mobile morgue. Down the line at Alpha Jeff's wife, Irene, waited past midnight to meet Jeff at the station, and from there they would go to the New Year's Eve Ball at the local hotel. Suddenly, we saw a pair of dazzled kangaroos dancing in front of the train, this way, that way, frantically searching for a way out of the tunnel of light

A train examiner at busy Rockhampton Station, favours an ice-cream over a cigarette during a "smoko" on the platform. The stylish stockman's hat he wears is standard issue throughout the tropical Queensland Railway network.

Top *Alone in his* Midlander *sleeping berth, Dick Menk, saddle and portable television set by his side, is on his way to Rockhampton for an operation for cancer.* **Above** *At Longreach Station, moments before departure, a grandfather, on his way home to Gympie, snatches one last kiss through the double-glazing of the train's window, as his grandchildren tearfully bid goodbye.*

THE MIDLANDER

created by the loco's beam. The kangaroos were lucky, but other beasts aren't as fortunate. A cow can be carved in half and hurled to the side of the track by the force of the locomotive, while some just disappear underneath the train.

At Alpha too, Lloyd's wife waited for him on the verandah of their house with a cold beer and a wish for the New Year. It was the first time in 45 years or so that he had missed a New Year's Eve.

"I'll get a kiss from the wife, whether I like it or not, I suppose," laughed Lloyd Vagg. Every 90 seconds he slapped the vigilance button, designed to keep the driver alert on long hauls. If the button was not struck, the lights would flash, horns would sound and the train's emergency brakes would automatically go on. Up ahead, somewhere in the blackness, the first lights of Alpha revealed themselves one by one.

"Jeez! I've been waiting for this moment all night," Jeff Clews said, as at last he embraced his wife on the platform of the station.

It was the end of the line for the engineman and the fireman. A fresh crew would replace them for the sector ahead. Together they saw in the New Year at the controls of a slow-moving train, halfway on a track that stretched almost the breadth of Queensland. At dawn, the wide open country of Longreach had disappeared during the night and the *Midlander* was trundling through gentle hills near Rockhampton. A sleeping berth contained Dick Menk, a German-born stockman from Queensland's Far West. He travelled alone, except for a television set and a riding saddle. For breakfast, he drank a bottle of beer.

"I shouldn't be drinking this, I suppose," he said, a Slim Dusty ballad gurgling in the background. "The doctors wouldn't like it, I suppose. I've got stomach cancer, you see. The chemotherapy didn't work. I'm going to Rockhampton for the operation."

CHAPTER FOUR
THE QUEENSLANDER

Inside the dining car of the *Queenslander*, as it rolled into the night, Arnie the American stabbed his Reef Fish Yeppoon with the fish knife that had suddenly become an unlicensed weapon in his hand. Here, across the table, was an angry man. Already he was incensed that his converted greenbacks hadn't bought him any sea views from the train, and now he was furious at discovering that Cairns was bereft of beaches but teemed with stingers, mudflats and skinflint back-packers. "For Chrissake!" he said, as the vase containing the pretend tropical flora wobbled gently on the table. "I paid big bucks for this train ride and you know what we get to see today? Nothin' but hills for Godsake! I expected to see water all the way. Now you guys tell me there's no friggin' beach in Cairns! You must be kiddin' me!"

A couple of kilometres further down the line and it was time for dessert. The choice was our first test: would it be Bowen Cheesecake, Bundaberg Bombe, Cooktown Delight Fruit Salad or the Queensland Cheese Platter? The waitress in the smock and the sour expression waltzed involuntarily down the aisle with Arnie the American's dessert, the Bombe—"Chocolate mousse flavoured with Queensland's favourite rum". His Texan wife, Rachael, suffering from an unpleasant outbreak of shingles ("It's the nerve ends, you know") demurely devoured the Cooktown Delight Fruit Salad—"Tropical fruit salad and ice-cream". The conversation had taken a violent detour to the complex issue of social welfare. Arnie the American had suddenly become an undetonated explosive. Rachael's slightly bloodshot eyes lolled in her head and, aware that a tirade was imminent, she scurried back to her compartment.

"You guys here in Australia haven't got any problems," said Arnie the American, a tall, middle-aged man with a dark beard flecked with grey, as he reclined in his chair. "The Bronx is worse than Calcutta, you know. The blacks don't even talk English any more. It's some kind of weird dialect. If I were

Between Brisbane and Rockhampton, electric-power lines propel rail traffic. Beyond the Rockhampton current and on to Cairns, trains like the luxury Queenslander, *revert to the customary diesel power.*

TICKET TO RIDE

President you know what I'd do? I'd ship 'em all back to Africa. We don't need 'em, for Chrissake!"

"Even Bryant Gumbel?" I asked cautiously. He replied: "That godamned son-of-a-bitch Liberal! He'd be the first to go! I'm a rabid right-winger and I don't mind who knows it. The United States is full of commies—and you guys in Australia had better watch out too. "You've got too many damned rules here. Everywhere we go there's signs saying things like 'Don't tie your shoelaces here,' 'Don't blow your nose there.' "

The faces of the dining car waitresses bore the fatigue of all those who have spent too long in the service of tourists, answering their absurd queries, enduring their outrageous complaints and taking orders for meals with silly names like "Rockhampton Roast". They ordered us, as we lingered over our coffee a little too long, to retire to the lounge car so they could retire. On the way there was a sign saying "No thongs, please." Arnie smirked and looked at me. "See what I mean?"

The Queenslander *about to leave Rockhampton Station for the final thrust in to the far-north.*

The *Queenslander*, all silver, gold and blue, is the flagship of the state's railway network. It was commissioned in 1986, in the languid pre-Fitzgerald Inquiry days, by the then Minister for Transport, Don Lane. A brass-band played and balloons were released and there was free champagne on every table.

When the *Queenslander* pulls away from Brisbane's Roma Street Station, Cairns is a day and a half away up the great stretch of coastline. The *Queenslander* is the "Sunshine State's" equivalent, so they contend, of the *Orient Express*, though its only real mystique was in the identity of the "surprise" filling inside the Breast of Chicken Cairns.

The scenery outside remained a secret too, for we had boarded the *Queenslander* for the night at Rockhampton, late on a Sunday afternoon after our arrival on the *Midlander* from Longreach. Undistracted by the vistas, we were cosy in the lounge car. Queensland Railways' marketing department had been valiant in its crusade to offer a train that might win back the legions lost to the skies. All the gloss might have tempted Minister Lane to rename the *Queenslander* as the "Peanut Impress" and be done with it. The first-class passenger on the *Queenslander*, for instance, is the recipient of such luxurious appointments as complimentary toiletries in the sleeping berth, a train manager ("Don't hesitate to contact him"), and dinner menus supplying realistic full-colour illustrations of koala bears and native flora, with valuable text. "The Cooktown Orchid has long been popularly regarded as Queensland's unofficial floral emblem. It was only in 1959, during celebrations to mark the state centenary, that the distinctive native plant was proclaimed Queensland's official floral emblem."

The Queenslander, *for the less privileged, is not all complimentary toiletries kits and plush dining cars. Down the back in economy, a couple of snoozing passengers have bought "sit-ups" for the arduous day and a half trip from Brisbane to Cairns.*

But the toiletries kit, embossed with an insignia of the *Queenslander*, was not well-received by everyone. "The toiletries kit will be the first to go, you mark my words," said the plump computer programmer from Melbourne, sipping yet another iced Coca-Cola in the lounge car. "They used to give you a route map on the *Indian Pacific*, but not any more. The *Queenslander*'s toiletries kit won't last six months before they drop it."

The bar in the lounge car was closed to prevent illicit forays on the alcohol rations after the strict closing-time. The barmaid had packed away her copy of *Australasian Post* and gone to bed. But resourceful Arnie the American, undeterred by this sudden deprivation, slipped away for a moment and materialised with a bottle of duty-free whisky stuffed under his body-shirt. The other passengers soon abandoned the lounge car when the alcohol supply dried up. Alone in the lounge car except for an Australian photographer with alternative political beliefs he had befriended over the Reef Fish Yeppoon that night, together they demolished the bottle and warred over politics until the early hours of the morning. I favoured discretion and, leaving Arnie and Michael to their binge, left to raid my toiletries kit. I fell asleep attempting to assemble the traveller's toothbrush that came apart in two pieces to preserve space in a crowded suitcase. It's the thought that counts.

The next morning I rolled over in my bunk and flicked the stud which kept the window-blind closed. The blind flew up, spun on the roll at the top and the unwelcome light of day drenched the berth. The "Peanut Impress's" public address system squawked and a woman's voice announced that the 7.30 am breakfast sitting would be served in the dining car.

The blackness of the night had dissolved and now I could see canefields and pineapple plantations merging with lush mountains. The canefields were criss-crossed by railway tracks. There were carriages on the lines with big, empty metal baskets lying dormant at deserted sidings. Tall stalks of cane waved in unison with the breeze. Although cold inside the train it was already steamy outside. The grass beside the track glistened in the light which was now diffused by a black cloud.

Above *An elderly Torres Strait Islander woman, left, with her daughter in the background. The further north the* Queenslander *trudged, the more varied the background of our fellow passengers.* **Left** *Not far from the township of Babinda, children frolic in the tepid waters of a creek, as the* Queenslander *creeps across a low-level trestle bridge. Inside the train, passengers ready themselves for disembarkation at Cairns, an hour or so away.*

The *Queenslander* clung to the coastline but the sea was concealed, much to Arnie's chagrin, by headlands. If he could have bribed someone to have them moved, I am sure he would have done so. We flashed past houses balanced on stilts, their protection against floods and heat. The tropics had been penetrated and the train was now in the steamier zone, full of exotica, that lies beyond the Tropic of Capricorn.

On a tourist train, time becomes the hours, minutes and seconds to the next meal in the dining car. At breakfast a couple of fellow diners, devouring strips of bacon that tasted like a deep-fried vinyl briefcase, had noticed the absence of the mysterious American woman and her two daughters from their allotted seats. At dinner the night before, they told me, she had surgically dissected her Rockhampton Roast of the Day—"Tender Central Queensland roast fillet of beef and sauce"—and decided that the food in the dining car was inedible and a serious health risk. With nationalistic zeal she located each American travelling on the train and warned them of the danger, then retired to her cabin never to be seen again. This self-appointed American health inspector had abandoned, in fact, a modest mobile food festival with delectably named dishes like Ravioli Innisfail, Fitzroy Fillet, Sunshine Salad and Cold Meat, and the remainder of the Cooktown Delight Fruit Salad.

It was video time in the lounge car, somewhere between Rockhampton and Mackay. The "hygienically-treated headsets so you can listen to the videos without disturbing fellow passengers" were, infuriatingly, scorned by the passengers. Around the television set there was a scrum ignoring the possibilities of spontaneous conversation, but immersed in a video movie called *The Henderson Kids*. Even aboard the train, one of the true last vestiges of the art of conversation had succumbed to the video age.

At the bar a hung-over Arnie the American was still discussing politics and downing impressive quantities of bourbon. Back in his Texan home town, Fort Worth, he owned a company which specialised in railway technology. He was watching the progress of the "Peanut Impress" with the focus of a bald eagle.

Already the computer programmer had bought himself from the bar a souvenir Queenslander T-shirt with a sketch of the train on the pocket—and another glass of Coke. The shirt seemed a size too small, considering how his stomach plunged over his lap and hid his shorts beneath his belly each time he sat down. I rashly told him I was travelling by train around Australia to write a book that would be published on my return, and bemoaned the demise of the many old trains, deemed financially unworthy, which had been replaced by buses. He sipped his Coke and peppered me with an astoundingly detailed list of the Australian rail routes, freight included, which had closed down. He was unstoppable, firing trivia-tipped bullets, and I squirmed in my seat. A woman nearby attempted to rescue me by changing the subject to the scenery outside, to no avail. It is unwise to make enemies in the confinement of a train, so I allowed him to complete his inventory. He ceased the discourse when I offered to buy him another Coke.

The Queensland railway network crawls with train enthusiasts. Almost invariably they travel alone. Few souls apart from their own brethren can

Top right *The torrid morning after the toxic night before. In his cabin on the* Queenslander, *Arnie the American momentarily forgoes his vigilance of the Queensland coastline in a vain quest for a hang-over remedy.*

Bottom right *A day and a half after it left Brisbane's Roma Street Station, the* Queenslander, *rinsed by a late-afternoon tropical storm, enters the outskirts of Cairns. A child surveys the final moments of one of the world's epic rail journeys.*

tolerate their scanning of the working timetables, their reminiscences of extinct rolling stock, their obsessive eye for detail and their love of souvenirs. If you watch closely you can see them at stations examining the train's underbelly, searching for an insignia, a plaque or inscription—any shred of information for yet another entry in pocket notebooks already bulging and frayed with railway trivia.

Intriguingly, rail-buffs almost never mention the travellers or scenery they encounter on their journeys. They will, however, produce the notebook and inform you of the exact length of the locomotive and the precise distance from one station to the next. If you chance to express even the most fleeting interest in trains they will corner you and bemoan the demise of half the nation's trains and supply the complex itinerary of their next trip.

But just like the trains they ride, rail-buffs are an endangered species. When the trains disappear—and the scales of economy dictate that one day they must—they will be left with only their pedantic notebooks, scale models and souvenir T-shirts. In the meantime, I had learnt my lesson never to confess an admiration for rolling stock.

On either side of the train the mountains separated and there at last lay Arnie the American's nirvana—the elusive Pacific Ocean. Arnie knelt on the lounge suite, as if in prayer, and the bristles of his greying beard pressed against the glass. Before long, the ocean vanished behind yet another headland but the American had been placated. He had seen the sea. Cairns, however, waited a few hundred kilometres up the meandering track and the crisis over mud flats, stingers and skinflint back-packers still loomed.

The Queenslander, *dwarfed by verdant peaks and flanked by rich grassland near Cairns, switches on its headlights to pierce the murkiness of the damp afternoon.*

The pride of Normanton, aside from the venerable Gulflander *itself, is the domed-roofed railway station, recently done up for its centenary.*

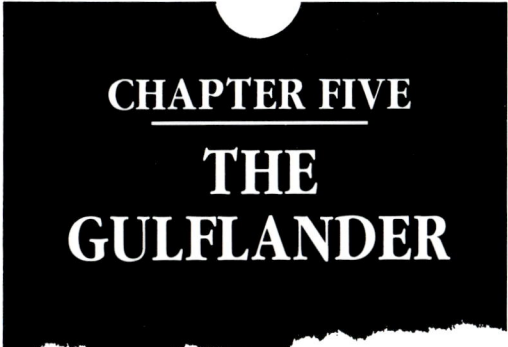

CHAPTER FIVE
THE GULFLANDER

A stranger, a long time gone, had returned to the Gulf of Carpentaria. The great arc of the wet had drenched the torso of the continent from one edge to the next and the dead country was alive again. Everywhere, as the heroic little train trudged down the track, the rivers had split their sides, the billabongs had broken their banks and the roads had become creeks. The same black clouds which frowned over the Gulf hung just as sternly over the *Gulflander*. Back at Queensland Railways' head office in Brisbane, a world away from the Gulf country, there were the annual mutterings that the chugging anachronism should be shut down forever. Yet nothing, however, can stop the *Gulflander*. Not even mere Acts of God. Ever faithful to its streamlined timetable, the *Gulflander* weekly leaves Normanton for Croydon, in the deep north-west corner of Queensland, down a rickety old line where strands of grass sprout between the splintery sleepers and all manner of wildlife hide in the scrub. The train recovers from the four-hour trip overnight in the railway yards at Croydon which only ever host one loco. The next morning, after a stolid breakfast in the dining-room of the Croydon Hotel, it changes direction and returns to Normanton, where it remains silent for another week unless it is chartered by picnickers. The few who stay overnight at Croydon to wait for the return trip are reminded to bring their darts for the Wednesday night tournament with the congenial whites and blacks in the Croydon Hotel's public bar.

On each occasion that the *Gulflander* embarks on another journey, it is in itself a singular feat of survival. When we passed through, an old canefields loco dolled-up for the ride with a weary carriage built in Sydney long ago was doing the job while the regular rail-motor was being restored at a Townsville workshop. During the intensity of the wet season the predominantly dirt road between Normanton and Croydon becomes a quagmire which is sometimes declared impassable for all but the most robust four-wheel drive vehicles and is sometimes closed to all traffic. It was for this reason that we were forced to fly to Normanton from Cairns. When the road is closed, the stranded

Top *A flurry of interest in the early morning at Normanton, as a couple of local children pedal down the street to the station to farewell the* Gulflander *on its weekly jaunt to Croydon.*   **Above** *Ready to go at Normanton Station: Col Shepherd, engineman, and his right-hand man, Patrick Wheeler.*

THE GULFLANDER

townsfolk and the remote station-owners who live beside the railway line seek their salvation from the *Gulflander*.

Not long after dawn on Wednesday, when the train departed for Croydon, Col Shepherd, the *Gulflander*'s laconic stationmaster, engineman, conductor and public relations officer, donned his crash-helmet and kick-started his motor scooter to ride down to the station. He took his usual lightly packed port, with his own set of darts inside, for the overnight stay at the Croydon Hotel; the only pub in town. It is famous, if not notorious, for its slipshod, lime colour scheme, flimsy corrugated iron walls, spartan guest rooms, bare wooden floors and—the biggest bugbear of all—wildly-inflated tariffs. A moment or so later, Shepherd was gliding down the street to the station, passing the occasional Aborigine still bleary from a night at the infamous purple-painted pub favoured by the local blacks. The ride on the scooter would be his last smooth trip for a couple of days. At 8.30 am, the *Gulflander*, its engine a spruced-up labour of love, materialised from beneath the grand white-domed roof of the old Normanton Station, which in the cooler, dry season lately has witnessed an unexpected influx of tourists who have heard of the little railway's immense charms.

Normanton Station has received lashings of whitewash over its former rusty visage, though there are diehards who favour the corroded version, and you can't blame them. The irony remains that although the tourists might rescue the *Gulflander* from closure, it is they who will diminish the enchanting uniqueness of the service. The *Gulflander* is *not* a tourist train and never has been—and that, essentially, is its appeal. But now it must draw the tourist trade to survive. At the oppressive height of the wet season, however, when tourists are discouraged by reports of enervating heat and flies the size of blue heelers, passengers on the *Gulflander* are rare. It was up this wild, uncharted Gulf of Carpentaria that even Burke and Wills suffered second thoughts.

By the time the train shed the meagre outskirts of one of the most isolated outposts in Australia, it had reached its modest cruising speed of just 30 km an hour; even slower along the more contorted sections of the track. Yet, even at this sluggish pace of life, the *Gulflander* was in a hurry. Among the passengers was a couple of phlegmatic, ill-humoured railway inspectors who had been dispatched from Hughenden on the Mount Isa line down south to assess the *Gulflander* and file a report on it. Yet there was little to assess—as long as the *Gulflander* made it to Croydon unscathed and unhurried and the passengers weren't tossed about by too many kinks, what else could matter? Just sit back and enjoy the ride for God's sake. The inspectors had wisely brought with them a four-wheel drive fitted with railway wheels, strapped to the flat-bed carriage, which they planned to attach to the railway line for the

The notoriously-contorted Normanton to Croydon rail-link—more kinks, so they say, than the average wife-swapping party.

The billabongs and rivers had burst their seams, but not even floods could stop the Gulflander *on its way to Croydon.*

Top *A mob of wild horses near Croydon is startled by the advancing* Gulflander's *rattle and hiss.* **Above** *A storm envelopes the fragile-looking* Gulflander *on its return journey to Normanton from Croydon.*

THE GULFLANDER

return trip to spare themselves a night at the Croydon Hotel. Elsewhere was the inspectors' driver and his chain-smoking wife, a perspiring fat woman in a floral dress whose tightly curled lips turned a disturbing shade of blue from the heat. Down the back were an Aboriginal man and his giggly, fat wife. In the brake van squatted Patrick, Shepherd's Aboriginal right-hand man, sorting the mail and supplies to be delivered to the handful of inhabitants along the line. And then there was Michael and I, sweaty and scarred from vicious mosquito bites.

Each journey for Shepherd is as proud a moment as the last. He loves the train and he loves the country it travels through. On the plodding route to Croydon, 150 km or so away, the *Gulflander* threaded its way through the seamless savannah country where brolgas danced one-legged on bulging waterholes and crocodiles snorkelled through muddied water. Halfway down the line a mob of horses splashed out of their billabong bath, alarmed at the advancing train's rattle and hiss. Besides the crocodiles lurking in the waterholes, the only real hazard along the way is the distorted track itself—more kinks, so they say, than the average wife-swapping party. The sound of the *Gulflander*'s ever-hissing brakes shattered the stillness of the scrub and stunned the cicadas, yet it might have been worse without Shepherd's intimate knowledge of the rogue kinks which twist the track like fresh strands of licorice. The kinks didn't, however, disturb the passengers, doped now by a heat-induced inertia, except for the blue-lipped red-faced fat woman who wobbled from side to side in her seat like an oversized raspberry jelly.

Along the track a gang of fettlers in battered ten-gallon hats were sipping boiling tea from a billy can as they waited for the *Gulflander*'s arrival. A tiny rail vehicle to carry the fettlers to the next kink, nicknamed the "Baby Gulflander", had been diverted to a siding to allow our passage. The *Gulflander* stopped for a chat anyway. It was these fettlers' unenviable task to maintain the distorted rails between the two towns and I was surprised at their gleefulness. A few minutes before we arrived at the camp they had sighted a pair of crocodiles freestyling in a nearby billabong, their eyes gliding across the surface in a gentle, though telltale ripple. The *Gulflander* stops sometimes for a moment or two so that Shepherd and Patrick can snack on the sweet wild berries that grow abundantly along the line, or perhaps to collect the odd antique bottle glittering in the scrub ditched during one of the *Gulflander*'s myriad incarnations.

During the gold rush that struck Normanton and Croydon during the 1880s, the notion of a railway line was mooted by the Queensland Inspector-General of the Railways, George Phillips. In 1888, construction began on a submersible line in the fickle flood-prone terrain. The line was completed three years later and four trains a week were scheduled to run between the two towns. When the gold fever subsided the line was plunged into a decline, interrupted only by the Gulf's development resurgence in the 1960s. The train became popular for its picnic and race meeting services.

A bit further down the line at Blackbull, one of a handful of stops along the way, Tanya Quirk, station-owner and mother of six, climbed out of her doorless truck, ready to receive the latest mail from the distant outside world. Although there was dirt smudged on her face, her hat was a little frayed and she wore a pair of manly shorts, there was an air of scruffy elegance about her. During the tourist season in the cooler months Quirk's enterprising children sell cake and cordial to the passengers who travel from all over the world for the four-hour train ride.

"We've been here seven years and the roads have been closed quite a few times, but the *Gulflander*'s never not got through in the wet," she said.

On a faded seat in the carriage the pages of the visitors' book were turned by a frail breeze. I found an entry by a Norwegian tourist written in a shaky hand, perhaps because of a kink Shepherd had failed to avoid. In the "comments" column the Norwegian had written: "One of the great little railways of the world". Although it was Shepherd's idea to place the visitors' book in the carriage, he hadn't noticed the comment.

The Douglas family aboard the Gulflander, *returning to Normanton after visiting relatives in Croydon.*

"Yeah, he's right, I suppose. The *Gulflander*'s got a bit a atmo', hasn't it?"

When the train finally returned to Normanton we would farewell the *Gulflander*. A taxi would be waiting to take Michael and me on to Mount Isa.

On congested city streets the cab driver's existence is a tortuous one. First, he must store a street directory, complete with cross-references, in his head. Then he must fight the foul-tempered radio operators who, back in the comfort of their base, squawk their incessant demands at him as he attempts to evade another maniac motorist or negotiate a sudden road hazard. Worst of all, he must engage in traffic warfare to survive. All that sort of nonsense is as alien to the Bush taxi-man as an unchilled twist-top. Out here, you wave at your fellow motorist as you pass each other—no big deal, just a brief elevation of four fingers while your thumb remains on the steering wheel. The two-way radio is blissfully silent and the only congestion is caused by bewildered cattle wandering into the taxi's trajectory. At the Albion Hotel in Normanton, the sort of old-fashioned outback pub where the only changes ever recorded are the dimensions of a drinker's pot belly, the boozers at the bar have nicknamed 28-year-old Greg Cummings "the Bush Taxi Man", an epithet he appears to revile and revere simultaneously.

Above *"Taxi! Can you take us from the Gulf of Carpentaria to Mount Isa, please?"* **Right** *When stock wander on to the roads, highway carnage results.*

THE GULFLANDER

On the road to Mount Isa, ignoring the turnoff to the tree on which Burke and Wills had practised a desperate form of woodwork before their lonely deaths, I reclined in the front seat of the Falcon, squirming on the vinyl upholstery as I realised this would undoubtedly be the most expensive taxi ride of my life. At Normanton we struck a serious dilemma. The next sequence of the trip would take us to Mount Isa—600 km of sparingly tarred, one-lane highway, inhabited exclusively by deceased fauna decaying by the road-side in a feast for flies. We planned to fly to Darwin the morning after our arrival in Mount Isa, for fear of the wet, make the long sweep down to Perth, and veer eastwards to complete our epic loop from Sydney and back.

The next train, in the meantime, would not emerge on our itinerary until Port Hedland on the other side of the continent. The skies above Normanton would not see the south-bound aircraft for days and hitch-hiking was an uncertain business during the wet season when the roads out of town are eerily empty. The last bloke who waited for a lift down south, so they say, got married and fathered six children in the interim. For the modern traveller, however, hope somehow always hovers on the horizon. It was in this vicinity of course, that even Burke and Wills began to seriously doubt their chance of deliverance to civilisation. Just when we began to suffer a similar attack of the tyranny of distance, a scheme suddenly occurred to us. If only the explorers could have hailed a taxi! Our last hope of salvation from the Gulf of Carpentaria was the local cab service. Far from anywhere in the Gulf country, few would be game enough to deny Cummings his title, for what it's worth, as one of the most far-flung taxi drivers on earth.

"When my wife and me went on holiday to Brisbane recently we caught a few cabs here and there," said Cummings as his cab glided down the road past thousands of giant anthills haphazardly ranging the landscape like brittle tombstones, and ripe from the rain.

"The one thing that really irritated me was the constant bloody chatter of the radio between the driver and the operator. You know the stuff: 'Are you there car 5? You out there car 6?' and all that. You don't get that sort of thing out here, no way. You're more likely to hear a Kevin Bloody Wilson tape."

For many of the local blacks, possibly his most valued customers, Cummings' taxi service is their sole means of transport around Normanton.

"On social security day I can get up to ten calls a minute. Most of the callers just get up and walk when they can't get through—there's only me and my wife, Toni. I have more trouble with the drunken whites than with pissed black fellas. They always pay up, no matter what."

In the Gulf of Carpentaria, there are no meters in the cab.

(67)

The bush-taxi man, Greg Cummings, on his longest flag-fall: from Normanton to Mt Isa.

"Hey, I don't even know what a bloody flag-fall is, to tell you the truth. The only reason we stick the taxi signs on the cab is so the locals don't mistake us for a cop car," he said. The fares were negotiated even before Cummings applied his foot to the accelerator. His average long-distance charge was between $100 and $200, though he had received few calls as demanding as our mission to Mount Isa, five hours or so away. The enormity

of the flagfall, however, left him untroubled. "No jolly problem" was his motto. He could afford to be carefree. The fare to Mount Isa, a town set between craggy mountains which might have once qualified as an idyllic setting before the intrusion of the spewing chimney stacks of one of the world's biggest silver, lead and zinc mines, was $500. The receipt, I thought, was worth framing.

CHAPTER SIX
THE IRON ORE TRAIN

Even before the speedometer had shattered the state speed limit it had become obvious that Barry and Geoff had been far too long in the company of their fellow miners. As the Falcon careered down the single-lane highway, with us in the back seat tightening our seat-belts in expectation of an impact, every third word was the four-letter one. They wore the word as proudly as a Victoria Cross.

Just after dawn, when the flies had risen for another day's confrontation with humanity, we had arrived at Barry and Geoff's stark workplace—a dusty lead, zinc and iron concentrate mine near Fitzroy Crossing. For a moment there, the Great Outdoors didn't seem so great any more. During the night we had hitched a ride on a road convoy from Wyndham, Western Australia's northernmost town, the place the crocodiles boycotted when the abattoir closed and the blood stopped flowing into the salt-pans. The fearsome machines, almost the size of a jumbo jet, were driven by congenial truckies who worked for a company called Gulf Transport. The machines might have been half the length of a football pitch, but there was little room for passengers. We had to squeeze into a tiny round cabin for the nine-hour trip from nowhere to nowhere, but it was a ride that kept us ahead of schedule and we seized it. Since most road-trains ignore hitch-hikers, we were lucky, though it was a restless night with hourly wake-up calls on the truckies' two-way radios.

"Your blokes asleep yet?" Squawk. "Yeah, think so . . ." Squawk. Still, they had been kind enough to give us a lift and we didn't want to appear ungrateful. Besides, I couldn't sleep after a disturbing experience in the roadhouse toilet along the way. A swarm of every conceivable breed of insect in residence under the neon light made the simple act of bowel release an excursion in terror as they buzzed their prey, the prisoner on the toilet seat.

The misery of the road-train was nothing compared to the horror of the coach (surely the most unedifying means of long distance transport ever

On the road between Wyndham and Fitzroy Crossing, Western Australia, road-train truckies, Jamie Cooper and Dick Kay, stop for an impromptu sunrise smoko, but are soon forced inside again by marauding bush-flies.

THE IRON ORE TRAIN

devised) we had taken a few days before in Darwin en route to Kununurra, an hour's drive from Wyndham. We were destined for Port Hedland to catch Australia's longest train a few thousand kilometres away. The first of the giant rigs, a carnival of orange and red warning lights which had left Wyndham at 10 pm and driven through the night, rolled into the mine to collect the first load of grey powder for the day. Here, yet again, we found ourselves at the end of the line and feared we might have to hail a taxi again. But then miraculously, two saviours materialised out of a cloud of thick grey dust—Barry and Geoff. They worked at the lead, zinc and iron concentrate one week on, one week off. It was their week off and, even better, they were going our way. The mine manager had asked them to return a hired car to their hometown, Derby, three and a half hours away and there was room for us.

"You blokes want a fuckin' lift to Derby, we hear," Geoff said as he braked the Falcon in a cloud of dust.

Barry, balding and bearded, was as eager to leave the mine as a man on parole. He packed his plywood model aeroplane into the boot of the Falcon with the care of a mother placing an infant in its cot. (The mine management had agreed to build a grass airstrip for the model plane enthusiasts among the miners. An artificial waterfall was being fashioned from a rocky outcrop beside the prefabricated miners' quarters.)

Barry slid into the front seat while Geoff, curly-haired with red stubble, seized the wheel and fired the ignition. In a willy-willy of gravel and dirt the car hurtled onto the highway. Here was proof that a Falcon could reach 150 km an hour in five seconds from a standing start.

"Fuck! I'm glad to be out of that fuckin' hole," sighed Barry, reclining in the front passenger seat with his chunky boots resting on the dashboard.

"Fuck, yeah," replied Geoff at the wheel. "Couldn't fuckin' wait! Put a fuckin' tape on, fuck you, Barry . . . Nice fuckin' car, eh?"

Just as the Falcon was tearing down the highway for take-off, Geoff gave the speedo a reprieve, for up ahead was the Fitzroy Crossing roadhouse. The roadhouse at Fitzroy Crossing, and the town itself for that matter, was as surreal a place as any this side of the equator. It appeared to be exclusively patronised by gnarled Aborigines in the saddest phase of decay. The preservation of the milk in the roadhouse refrigerator was more successful, judging by the expiry dates I found there. It turned out that Fitzroy Crossing was so far from any significant population centre that the milk arrived snap-frozen from down south, several thousands of kilometres away. Barry and

Checking his rig on the road to Fitzroy Crossing: Gulf Transport truck driver, Dick Kay.

Geoff counselled that the milk was "perfectly fucking safe to drink" though it was impossible to reconcile this with expired expiry dates, and I chose dehydration over a strawberry shake.

On a previous visit to Fitzroy Crossing a young black man had offered me his sister's chastity on the idyllic banks of the Fitzroy River for $10, as nearby a pair of teenage boys brawled in the caking red dirt, their limbs waving like a couple of frenzied praying-mantis. On this, my less than triumphant return visit, everyone was still doped from a night on the turps—or maybe they were just recovering from the sheer terror of waking up to another day at Fitzroy Crossing.

"Fuckin' tax dollars everywhere," Geoff sniffed irritably as the Falcon wove away from the roadhouse. The remark kept me puzzled. But then it occurred to me he was referring to the Aborigines.

Barry and Geoff en route to Derby.

"Yeah, fuckin' bloody tax dollars," said Barry, drinking his chocolate milk. The blacks scrambled out of the path, clutching their carbon-dated iced coffees as the Falcon skidded back to the highway. Out on the gun-barrel open road again the car, now edging the speedometer to where the little red arrow had never ventured, overtook a four-wheel drive crammed with Aborigines. The sight of the blacks crammed like sardines into the tray of the utility offended Geoff.

"If that many fuckin' whites were squashed into a fuckin' car that size the cops would be down on 'em like a fuckin' ton of bricks."

"Fuck oath," said Barry, shaking his head at the blacks as we passed them. They were wisely hanging on tight to the ute's roll bar and ignored his sneers.

At Derby, Barry and Geoff planned to get drunk, shoot pigs, chat up the nurses seconded from Perth to the prefabricated base hospital and maybe even sleep. They were Derby born and bred and deeply proud of their birthright. They loved the place. There was, of course, so much to do there. When the road turned into a giant fork, the car abandoned the highway and veered onto the road leading into the township. At the Boab Hotel—named after the local tree, so fat and hollow that the locals used to store prisoners inside them—we bade farewell to Barry and Geoff.

"Yeah, see you fuckin' later," said Barry, as Geoff applied the accelerator for maximum thrust.

Although we were mere itinerants who could leave at a moment's notice, I found it impossible to dislike the blacks. I remember how Michael, cameras dormant for a moment, sat alone under a tree across the road from the Boab Hotel while I ate lunch in the air-conditioned coolness with the locals who

A common sight in the iron-rich Pilbara region of Western Australia. A four-wheel drive vehicle, with railway bogeys attached, clamps on to the railway line between Port Hedland and Newman for a swifter passage.

would have rather I, too, had chosen the tree. A few minutes later I glanced out the window and he was joined by a couple of Aborigines squatting on the ground. They had seen a smiling white face and had come for a chat. A few minutes later I glanced out the window again. They had multiplied—and multiplied, until an impromptu corroboree had evolved amid much laughter.

The next day, another thousand kilometres or so away, we waited high above the Pilbara region of Western Australia on a mountain-top littered with cracked volcanic rock, while a steel snake slithered from behind an escarpment on the far side of the valley. The rumble of its body (the length of an average city street) was almost smothered by the whistle of the hot breeze. It seemed forever before its 240 carriages curled around the winding track and disappeared down the rails. It was a spellbinding sight. From this lookout, halfway between Port Hedland and Newman, David O'Neill had

High above a Pilbara valley, framed by the rugged Chichester Ranges, David O'Neill surveys one of his massive 240 carriage iron-ore trains weaving its way to Newman.

surveyed his unlikely kingdom. Behind the ridge was his home, the Mount Newman Mining Company railway camp called Redmont—not far from Marble Bar, one of the hottest spots in the country where temperatures reach 50°C—at the feet of the Chichester Ranges and more or less the intermediate point along the 426 km of track.

Since the line opened in 1969, trains have hauled over 500 million tonnes of ore along it from the port to Mount Whaleback, the vast iron ore mine at Newman. The longest private railway in the country and one of the world's most extensive, it takes eight hours to complete the trip between the two centres. In one year Mount Newman Mining trains pull more tonnage than all the freight of the public state networks combined. The tireless, orange-painted Mount Newman Mining locomotives—two up the front and a couple more in the middle for additional power—can pull 25,000 tonnes of iron ore

(which in extracted form resembles curry powder) in as many as 240 carriages which stretch for 2.5 km. A mishap down the back causes more dread than doomsday because the company can lose thousands of dollars if a track is blocking traffic, and drivers like Tom Donkin and Roger Sherwood can expect an hour's round trip by foot to inspect the problem. The 100 km on either side of Redmont is O'Neill's domain. Each day a small though significant portion of the gross domestic product flows through his control. What he has built himself at Redmont is an oasis compared to the choking artificiality of Port Hedland and Newman.

"Out here at Redmont you get away from politics and bullshit," he said, surveying the view around him. "There's areas of the Pilbara, you know, where you'd swear to Christ you're in South Africa."

O'Neill is married, with two teenage children who live at Redmont and are educated by correspondence. He met his wife, a former governess, in South Australia one night beside a railway line he was inspecting. The governess, waiting for a train in cold darkness, had made a fire with some railway sleepers. He abused her for destroying the sleepers and they didn't meet again for several months.

Redmont railway camp: an authentic oasis in the depths of the Pilbara.

On a rail that can become hot enough to press a shirt collar, fettler Stan Lloyd rests after an exhausting bout on the hammer and spike.

At Redmont at knock-off time the "wet mess" was fully operational. It was refreshing to learn that we had not left the swearing completely behind. A Swedish visitor to the wet mess had left the barman a $50 tip because, he explained, he enjoyed the swearing so much. The railway camp at Redmont was just about the only place in the Pilbara where the atmosphere between workmates had not been chilled by a particularly bitter industrial dispute by Mount Newman Mining workers. I noticed that a huge man in an orange headband still damp from the sweat of a tough day's toil was drinking fearsome quantities of Emu Export. In the bar he was nursing his "railway baby" (a son born at Redmont called Kaz) in arms thick as concrete railway sleepers. His name was Janusz Wroblewski. He was a "ganger", a foreman on a team of railway fettlers whose task it was to maintain the rails which become so hot during the day you could press a shirt collar on them. The heat is so intense that one of his fellow fettlers, a man with fair skin, returned to camp with legs so sunburnt they developed sores overnight and earned him the nickname "Blisters".

"I tell you what," Janusz said, peeling the ring-pull off another can, "you really sort the men from the boys when you get them on the hammer and the spike out here. It gets so hot up here in summer that, fair dinkum, there's only three of us who can take our shirts off without keeling over. When I got hired in Perth I said to them: 'Three years minimum and five years maximum.' Now

A dawn-patrol of Redmont fettlers attack the rails before the arrival of the first train and to evade the noon heat that often reaches 50°C.

Top *The foreman of the Redmont fettlers, Janusz Wroblewski, wearing his trademark head-band, nurses his "railway-baby" boy Kaz, beside the Port Hedland to Newman line.*
Above *Andy (Blisters) Shores, a fettler, takes a dip in the therapeutic waters of "the Resort", nestled in the Chichester Ranges.*

look at me. I'm still here seven-and-a-half years later. But I reckon I might get out soon, depending on the state of my finances. I wouldn't mind 30 acres by the sea somewhere, maybe Queensland."

It was at Newman that Janusz met his girlfriend, Janet. She later became a cook at the Redmont mess and ever since they have lived together in a prefabricated house at the camp. Before O'Neill took over the administration of the camp, women were not permitted there, but O'Neill convinced the hierarchy that a female element in the population—normally no more than 100 or so workers—would civilise Redmont. Since then there have been several marriages. A party of fettlers was bound for Perth the next weekend for a workmate's wedding. The arrival of families has brought a sense of permanence to Redmont. One of the first innovations O'Neill made when he took over was to cease referring to Redmont as a camp. The management adopted the euphemism "track centre". The word "camp", O'Neill insisted, instilled the workers with the notion that they were merely itinerants who could leave when the sun grew too hot. The workers can still leave, but now they would not be just abandoning a camp, but leaving a fully-fledged community.

At dawn the next morning the memory of Geoff's attempt to break the world land speed record had been rendered laughable by Janusz in the orange four-wheel drive. At least the roads Geoff tackled in his attempt were straight—and sealed. Inside the four-wheel drive Janusz's giant right foot was jammed on the accelerator. We were hurtling along at 130 km on a dirt road with deep dips and violent curves, on our way to "the Resort" high in the Chichester Ranges.

One day Janusz had had a vision. He found a couple of billabongs in the hills which were concealed from the railway line. Slowly, "the Resort" evolved. The fettlers began to buy goldfish and perch from a pet shop in Port Hedland, released them into the billabongs, and then fed them until they grew fat. In their spare time the fettlers built a kind of gazebo to eat their lunch, fenced the area off from wandering cattle and then basked in their achievement. When anyone mentions "the Resort" to O'Neill he just shakes his head and laughs, though you know he admires the fettlers' whimsical enterprise. Now "the Resort's" fishpond population is bigger than Redmont's and Janusz has a new scheme—to plant cotton palms and create an artificial beach with sand from a quarry over the ridge. At the moment the fettlers have to slide into the water for a swim on the pads of conveyor belts so they don't burn themselves on the scorching rocks. Janusz seemed to regard "the Resort" as his legacy to Redmont when he finally leaves. In the uncertain meantime, it has served as a humanising retreat for some of the toughest workers in one of the toughest outposts in Australia.

CHAPTER SEVEN
THE INDIAN PACIFIC

It was not long after dawn at Kalgoorlie Railway Station and the sun was only squinting on the horizon. Even so, before the *Indian Pacific* had pulled away from the platform you could see that all its transcontinental pilgrims were either fatigued, decayed, or dumbstruck. Undaunted, I boarded the shiny silver canister and squeezed past the elderly woman with the bad back who was sidling down the narrow passageway like a wrinkled lobster.

In the sleeping car I located my twinette berth, dropped my suitcase on the seat, which at night would transform itself into a bed, and rushed off the train to catch a bus. During the half-hour stopover at Kalgoorlie, with droopy eyelids in dire need of scaffolding, the transcontinentals staggered aboard the Gold Rush Tours' coach awaiting them on the concourse outside, ready to convey them on the regular $5-a-head crash-course on the historical, cultural and scenic wonders of the famous gold-mining town that was offered to all interested passengers of the *Indian Pacific*.

"On your right, ladies and gentlemen," the coach captain and tour guide announced into his microphone headset, as the bus slowed for a better view, "is the first swimming pool built in Kalgoorlie—now a kindergarten."

On the homeward leg to the railway station we made a detour that was a trifle leisurely considering that one of the great trains of the world was idling impatiently, ready to resume its heroic journey. However, we made the inevitable visit to the infamous Hay Street, possibly the country's most concentrated half-kilometre of prostitution outside Kings Cross and St Kilda. Here, where the prostitutes still ply their nocturnal trade, was the lurid red-light district now dormant in the light of day. Gone were the girls who at night emerge for the seedy vigil where they sit and wait in tiny "dog-boxes"

An Australian dream fulfilled—to ride the Indian Pacific. *A passenger rises early from her twinette berth to view the fringe of the Nullarbor beyond Kalgoorlie.*

The Prospector, *the train which conveyed us from Perth, waits at Kalgoorlie Railway Station.*

not unlike backyard latrines and fashioned from scraps of corrugated iron with a bunk out the back. Gone too was the sordid parade of cars, their headlights dimmed, which anonymously prowl the wide street to make their shadowy selections.

"When the new madam took over the brothel on your right, ladies and gentlemen," said the guide, who wore a clinging white body-shirt over a white singlet. He cleared his throat and said, "She erected a sign which read 'Under New Madam-ment'—but the local police made her take it down."

The still semi-conscious pilgrims chortled wearily through their stubble, but their minds were back on the *Indian Pacific*. Already they were craving the tinned fruit-compôte which awaited them in the double-glazed dining car for breakfast, so they were unprepared for the sudden change of emphasis in the rambling, though informative, commentary.

"I neither condemn nor condone what goes on here," the bus driver said earnestly, his voice deepening for effect. "But there are 9,000 single men in this town and we have no rapes here."

At 6.30 am, inside the *Indian Pacific*, an unwelcome, nasal voice over the public address system alerted snoozing passengers and pilgrims just back from the Kalgoorlie tour that the first sitting of breakfast would promptly commence in the dining car at 7 am. I wondered if the shock of the raucous announcement could be perilous to pilgrims sleeping on the top bunks. It was, after all, a sheer drop to the floor below. For those unfortunates allotted the third sitting at 9 am, further sleep was impossible. On the hour, announcements were issued with the brutality of an army barracks. The only solution was to muffle the speaker with a pillow.

Darryn Milne waits at Kalgoorlie Station for his girlfriend from Perth.

At the second breakfast sitting, as we grimly scoured the train for signs of intelligent lifeforms and waved goodbye to the last trees before the onslaught of the Nullarbor, it seemed our only chance for idle conversation rested uneasily with two young Japanese men, Satoshi and Takashi. They wore T-shirts emblazoned with incomprehensible messages in English. The Japanese don't mind if T-shirt messages make no sense at all, as long as the message is in the boldest English lettering. The waiter, in a uniform of bright blue vest, crisp white shirt, bow tie and black trousers with a stripe down the side, sat us beside them. The woman behind us, waiting for her first glimpse of the fruit-compôte, stared wistfully out the window at the fringe of the Nullarbor Plain.

"Oh, I wouldn't fancy living out there," she said to no-one in particular. By the end of our interlude on the *Indian Pacific* the statement would become a mantra, reverberating wherever we wandered.

Unfortunately, Satoshi and Takashi's joint command of English was as rudimentary as our knowledge of the intricacies of origami. Although they were officially mourning the death of the Emperor, they were still amiable enough to erase any residual Hirohito resentment among the train's battalion of Second World War veterans. But we understood, through sign language, that Satoshi had caught the train at "Purse" and that they were travelling to "Sinny", from where they intended to explore the hinterland on rented motor-bikes.

Undefeated, we pursued the unpursuable until Satoshi, giggling, revealed a miracle of the electronic age. It was a veritable pocket foot-bridge for spanning alien cultures; a pocket translator programmed to communicate basic, though essential, conversation in Japanese, Italian, French, German, Spanish and English. When Satoshi pressed a button, a myriad Japanese characters flickered onto the screen, followed by an unfailingly polite *English* translation.

"Excuse me, what do you recommend from the menu?" the device asked, as Satoshi smiled, pointing to the crystal lettering on the screen. He wildly nodded to encourage a response. In the not surprising absence of sashimi, I pointed to the menu's bacon and eggs. We somehow deciphered that Satoshi and Takashi were students of electronics in Japan, now adventuring in Australia, but we feared that if the worst happened and they lost the translation device, they too would be lost. We left them in the dining car just as Takashi, courtesy of the translator, asked us the name of the most popular film of the day, with the cutlery clinking softly from the gentle motion of the train. At last, the pocket tourist-guide had realised its potential.

It was still 1970 on the *Indian Pacific*. The food on the menu was 1970 food; the stewards looked like 1970 stewards; the passengers still dressed in 1970 fashions; the furniture was 1970; the announcements on the public address system were like those you might have heard in 1970. Only the organ was contemporary. The fact that we were locked in a kind of time-capsule was, in itself, not entirely a *bad* thing. From what I can recall, 1970 wasn't so bad a year. But nostalgia can be tedious if the era recalled is still too recent to feel emotional about. I decided to enjoy 1970 while it lasted because 1989 was just around the corner.

When tiny railway communities, just a handful of houses scattered along the line, started to appear by mid-morning, the personality of the train had evolved. During our journey around Australia I had gradually realised that the true identity of a train was not necessarily determined by the creature comforts it offered, nor the scenery for that matter, but the quality and variety of the company it carried. It was a lottery worth playing, but one that could often be riddled with bad fortune.

A meal sitting in the Indian Pacific's *dining car offers an unexpected juggling and balancing act, as waiters, laden with bleakly-traditional Australian fare, defy the unpredictable rhythms of the train.*

After a night on the train from Perth, the bulk of the Trans-continentals revealed themselves in the comfort of the lounge car as sprightly senior citizens with little to offer apart from hour upon hour of relentless pleasantries, as unremitting as the symmetry of the railway track beneath us. Some, by now, had even recorded sufficient kilometres for developing a contempt for one another.

The Indian Pacific *pauses on the straightest section of railway track in the world—not a curve for 498 km between the Nullarbor outposts of Nurina and Ooldea.*

At lunch, Perth's Grace, who remembered Bob Hawke as a boy ("He was arrogant, bumptious . . .") was seething over her apple crumble. At breakfast, she had quietly insisted to the waiter that she please not be seated next to the butcher's wife from Adelaide at lunch. Something unpleasant had occurred overnight and left a nasty taste in Grace's mouth. But first, the request had to be considered by the head waiter because it offended the train's protocol. A

Top On the Indian Pacific, Satoshi (left) and Takashi, solve the mysteries of an Australian railway breakfast menu with the help of their trusty translator. **Above** The view from the lounge car of the Indian Pacific is always the same.

passenger's seating allocation in the dining car is as firm as a set of handcuffs for the rest of the trip. If you and your dining partners didn't hit it off, you were stuck with the entire three days between Perth and Sydney or vice versa. It was a chilling prospect, though the brave could challenge the train etiquette and ask for a key to unlock the cuffs. The possibility of a bloodthirsty food-fight and the interests of passenger morale provoked the head waiter, tweaking his bow-tie nervously, to relent and grant Grace her unusual request.

Grace's partially deaf husband was either unperturbed by or oblivious to the broiling animosity between Grace and the butcher's wife who, I noticed ruefully, had been seated next to the Japanese men. Satoshi and Takashi had produced the pocket translator which seemed to confound the butcher's wife. John, Grace's husband, had a smile for everyone. He grinned at the scenery, he grinned at us and he grinned at his double serving of dessert.

"He doesn't look as sick as he is, does he?" Grace asked and of course I replied: "No, not at all." Any false move and Grace might request yet another seat allocation. Secretly, I suspected that John was, in fact, on the verge of senility or at the very worst, a rail-buff. He certainly bore the glazed appearance of one. Since the Melbourne computer programmer on the *Queenslander*, we had travelled thousands of kilometres without being harassed by the worst kind of rail-buff, and I vowed that we would maintain our track record, so to speak.

The Perth couple had booked, months ahead, the biggest roomette on the train for their fifth ride on the *Indian Pacific*, and they invited us to make a tour of inspection. It contained a couple of chairs and a desk, a bigger wardrobe, and room to stretch tired old legs on a long trip. The decor had clearly not been revised since the 1970s, but it *had* been slept in by royalty and prime ministers. Now it hosted a frail couple who had once owned a Perth service station where a boyish Bob Hawke used to inflate the tyres on his push-bike. It was an anecdote, I detected, produced by Grace and John for all strangers like us.

The plight of John's mysterious ill-health reminded me that almost everyone we had met on the *Indian Pacific* were prepared, at the veritable drop of a Medicare card, to volunteer their ailments in vivid detail. Except for Takashi and Satoshi, who were fighting fit (though their constant use of the pocket translator had exposed them to repetitive strain injury), all were battling some heinous illness. Not even a wartime hospital train could have carried this many walking wounded. You had to admire them all. The aged transcontinentals were infirm, but intrepid.

Yet despite their obvious allegiance to train travel, senior citizens, however nimble, loyal and welcome they might be, pose perhaps the greatest threat to the precarious future of the railways. Senior citizens travel at half-fare, but the railways desperately need to attract full-paying customers to reduce their escalating losses. The annual report on the *Indian Pacific* is a distressing tome of multi-million dollar losses.

Back in the lounge car in the afternoon, the transcontinental mantra—"Oh, I wouldn't fancy living out there"—was being recited with renewed vigour as we passed more depressed settlements, some of which had been wisely abandoned. I spied the butcher's wife, her lips crinkling with suspicion and disapproval at a couple of young American women sitting close together on a nearby lounge, scrawling postcards to friends back home. She suspected, I was convinced, that the women were more than just extremely close travelling companions. The answer to the mystery remained as frustrating as the identity of the killer on the *Orient Express*.

Above *A cyclist glides across the overhead footbridge at Kalgoorlie Railway Station at dusk* **Right** *Waiting for the* Indian Pacific *to arrive at Kalgoorlie Railway Station: 5.45 am.*

A rotund, retired Canadian with heart trouble, positioned in the middle of the carriage for an optimum view, resembled one of those sea-lions his compatriots beat to death with baseball bats. He confided that he had paid a lot of money to cross the world and ride the *Indian Pacific*. All he had got for his dollars was nothing—literally. But he was delighted by this particular nothing that existed out the window. In fact, he regarded it as the finest nothing a tourist could buy and you couldn't help but agree.

Although tattier these days, the *Indian Pacific* still occupies the top shelf of the Australian psyche since it was commissioned in 1970. It is, true enough, one of the great train journeys of the world, straddling the continent boldly from one seaboard to another. The route boasts the longest straight track anywhere in the world—not a curve (except for the odd kink caused by the baking sun)—for the 498 km between the railway communities of Nurina and Ooldea. It takes 65 hours to complete the epic 4,000 km journey. It is not difficult to see why Australians so affectionately speak of the *Indian Pacific* as a once-in-a-lifetime experience, though few make the journey since the fares compare unfavourably with an airline ticket.

From the window of the lounge car, where the tables had holes cut in them so passengers could leave their drinks without fear of spillage, an electronic organ moaned a computerised version of *Tea For Two*—hands-free at the flick of a switch. At that point I reassessed my satisfaction at knowing I would take to my grave an experience of the *Indian Pacific*. It was all a terrible disappointment, this musical accompaniment. All the footage I had seen of the *Indian Pacific* had shown gay old times where perky pilgrims

A respite in the lounge car of the Indian Pacific, *the hand-free electronic piano and its automatic rendition of "Tea For Two" in a brief abeyance.*

crowded around a real, tinkling-ivories *piano* for jolly sing-alongs in bicoastal comradeship as the train crawled across the country devoid of a care in the world. All we got was an antagonising, pre-programmed *Tea For Two* with optional drum-beat, at the flick of a switch.

The fat Canadian was still transfixed at the Nullarbor hoping to spot a kangaroo so that he wouldn't have to fib in the postcards he planned to send back to his hometown, Vancouver. But he needn't have bothered. The terrain wasn't going anywhere. Perhaps it resembled Mars, though it was hard to conceive how any self-respecting Martian could declare the Nullarbor habitable. The dwindled populous along the line might not have found the Nullarbor Plain habitable either—but they lived there, nevertheless. When the good Lord created the Nullarbor there must have been some sort of austerity campaign. "Oh, I wouldn't fancy living out there," someone muttered to the remorseless groan of *Tea for Two*.

Over the border of Western Australia, into South Australia and another time-zone, the *Indian Pacific* arrived at Cook, the famous Nullarbor settlement. At the station, just as we arrived, I met a train examiner called Henry Cox who was squatting, cigarette in mouth, outside a telephone box. He was toothless and the cigarette he was puffing was a roll-your-own. A transcontinental was using the telephone while Cox waited to ring his "skin and blister" (his sister), in Adelaide. He had little affection for the transcontinentals of the *Indian Pacific* and despite their presence around him, wasn't scared to admit it in a loud voice.

One of them once asked Cox how the settlement received its supplies. A mate of Cox's whispered in the man's impressionable ear that there was a deep-water port just a short drive down the track.

"Oh really? Is there a taxi? Do you think we'd have time to go and take a look?" he asked. The closest stretch of water to Cook is, of course, the Great Australian Bight a few hundred kilometres south, and the nearest major anchorage is Whyalla.

"If you really want to know, these passengers on the *Indian Pacific* are like bloody pelicans—always complaining about this, always complaining about that. Not all of 'em, mind you, but bloody most of 'em anyway. They should have two classes on the *Indian Pacific*, idiot class and moaner class if you ask me," said Cox. "I'd just been doing some brake-testing when I saw this bloke who had his hand on the bloody engine, and he said to me, 'Pardon me, is this the engine of the train or is it down the back?' Yeah, well, I said, 'Well, it's not a bloody Volkswagen, fella.' "

CHAPTER EIGHT
THE TEA AND SUGAR

On the fringe of the Nullarbor Plain, full of desolate sandhills which westwards dissolve to a defoliated nothingness, a dawdling parade of mismatched carriages creaked to a halt in a siding where we awaited an unlikely midnight rendezvous. A gentle, cool breeze fanned the blackened plain which was lit faintly by a half-moon suspended in a freckled sky of the eeriest clarity. The lumbering *Tea and Sugar* train had arrived at Barton, now dormant in the night.

A plumber who fixed the pipes of the tiny communities along the line had warned us that in the depths of the night there were secret perils on the Nullarbor. Beware, he warned, the ghost of the house-painter who died suddenly in the now abandoned "room six" at Barton, and who, on the way to the airstrip, sat bolt upright in his coffin, rigor mortis and all, after he had been declared as dead as the treeless plain itself. Beware, too, the spirit of Aeroplane Jack, the Aboriginal who would alight the *Tea and Sugar* and mysteriously overhaul the train by the time it arrived at the next stop. There Aeroplane Jack would be waiting on the platform, to the bafflement of all, nonchalantly puffing on a cigarette. Although the plumber swore to the authenticity of the legends, we had survived the terrors of the *Indian Pacific* and, emboldened with those credentials, I told him the ghosts could go and get exorcised. We were ready for anything. It seemed ludicrous that the *Indian Pacific* had conveyed us from one distant edge of the Nullarbor Plain to the next and now we found ourselves retracing the route directly the other way. Yet from inside the passenger train, those desperate-looking settlements we had plotted from the comfort of the lounge car had remained for most of us just perplexing blurs. It was safe and comfortable on the *Indian Pacific* and the bar had beer in the fridge when we wanted it. But it was frustrating, too—you could only marvel and wonder about the endurance of those who lived out there. The solution was to meet the *Tea and Sugar* train at the

The Tea and Sugar *lies idle in a siding on the Nullarbor between the settlements of Barton and Watson.*

railway community of Barton, just a handful of sturdy wooden homes facing the track and little else, and named after Australia's first Prime Minister. The *Tea and Sugar* was our ticket to the queer world that existed beyond the double-glazed windows of the *Indian Pacific*.

Once a week the *Tea and Sugar*—officially Slow Mixed Goods Train Number 4205—departs on its lonely, plodding and unique expedition from Port Augusta, South Australia, to Kalgoorlie, to inject morale into the isolated inhabitants of the Nullarbor Plain railway settlements. Nowadays the discarded wooden sleepers decay beside the track, replaced by indefatigable concrete successors which the railways hope will last half a century and slash their

A fettler on the Nullarbor prepares to unload strands of track.

crippling maintenance bills. The role of the fettler has been diminished by the advent of concrete.

The wooden sleepers lay beside the track, waiting for some ingenious entrepreneur to devise a smart method to collect and sell them for profit back in the city. Many of the existing settlements (52 once, now just a dozen or so) have been abandoned since the demise of the wooden sleeper. Next to go will be the crews from Telecom, constructors of a complex fibre-optic communications link between Adelaide and Perth. They have bolstered the Nullarbor population for a few years, but will leave it sagging when they pack up for home.

Bill (Brass) Willis stands beside the Tea and Sugar between Barton and Watson: "Jeez look at those forests out there . . . lovely mountains, too."

THE TEA AND SUGAR

One day soon the Nullarbor will be as deserted as ever it has been since the railways early this century penetrated the natural barrier between the west and the east. Even today the Nullarbor is an impediment between the two seaboards, though one might argue that it imposes more a tyranny of *psyche* than a tyranny of *distance*. It's as though the spirit of progress had arrived on the Nullarbor with intentions to stay, suffered second thoughts, turned back and made for civilisation way down the line.

The old days have faded like the paint-job on the *Tea and Sugar*'s carriages. Once a butcher in full regalia slaughtered the livestock in a butcher van on the way, but that's gone now. Today the freshest meat is the frozen packaged variety that can be purchased from the well-stocked retail van, a mobile general store and the real focus of the *Tea and Sugar*, which is fastened to the train for each weekly expedition. Every second week a bank van is attached and paymasters distribute wages to workers along the way. There are the "gins" too, giant tanks balanced on bogeys with 40,000 litres of water to quench the thirsty settlements and ensure the continuity of daily showers for the Plain dwellers. Every month or so a community service carriage bears a social worker with an ear to listen to the problems of isolation, depression, child-rearing and marriage, or just to chat. There is also the unfortunately-dubbed "boong van", primarily for Aboriginal travellers who wish to ride between intermediate stops, plus a variety of flat-bed carriages bearing fresh rails for the track. An infrequent traveller on the *Tea and Sugar* is the Reverend Noack, who climbs aboard the train at Easter, July and October, faithful to his lifelong crusade of warning the Nullarbor dwellers to renounce their wicked ways. It's impossible to conceive anything else quite like the *Tea and Sugar*.

"I miss the old days," said the guard, Neil Hamilton, between yawns. "Bloody oath, I do. There was a lot more to do on the line then. There were more people out here. The work of the guard is a lonely one nowadays. There'd always be a couple of decent blokes on board to have a nice old chat. In them days you'd stay overnight at the settlements and fraternise with the locals. All that's gone now . . . sad to say."

It was beyond midnight now. Inside the guard's van, with comfortable large sleeping berths and a bed which for once was actually fastened to the floor and not suspended from the wall, I slurped my coffee and bid goodnight to Neil and Bill Willis, a former stationmaster nicknamed Brass (as in bold as brass). He was along for the ride from Port Augusta and was instructed to keep an eye on us.

Inside my cosy mobile bedroom I switched off the dim light and thought of the painter who died on the Nullarbor. What a terrible fate, I thought, to die in hell, which is how the Nullarbor struck me. His sole legacy was a legend that he sat up in his coffin on the way to the airstrip where his body was to be transported back to civilisation. There was much death out there. Not in the human sense, but in the lifelessness of the country itself. Despite the clear skies, a cloud of gloom seemed to hang perpetually over the Nullarbor and it struck me as unlovable as anywhere could ever be. But it *was* compelling and I felt privileged to see it. I drifted to sleep, the slumber intermittently shattered by violent jolts each time the *Tea and Sugar* shunted to allow a freight train to progress on a more critical mission. The shunting stopped after a time, and there was suddenly a hollow, disturbing silence, one I had not experienced since we left Central Station on that far-away rainy Boxing Day afternoon almost a month before.

The following morning the train was moving again and Brass was in the guard's van kitchen, staring out the window at the treeless plain and sipping a milky cup of tea. He was in a sardonic mood.

"Jeez, look at those forests out there. Bloody beautiful. Lovely mountains, too," he said, deadpan. The train jerked and stopped. I poked my head out the window and saw in the distance, at work on the track, a gang of fettlers decked out in vivid orange vests and torn jeans through which bums were visible. It is a grim trade, the fettler's life. No joviality, just the clanking sound of the replacement rails tumbling to the track from the disconnected car of the *Tea and Sugar* and the familiar tedium of a laborious job that must be done. The hammers and the spikes flew in the air, gripped by strong hands, and the clank of iron struck upon iron echoed between the walls of the sandhills.

The fettlers, deprived of unlimited booze, television, radio and women, could be a fearsome bunch, a rag-tag assortment of losers, outcasts, ex-cons, family men not afraid of back-breaking work, and the faithful types who merely lived for the railway life. Not long ago, so they say, a fettler was found in a compromising position in the bedroom of a fellow fettler's wife by her husband, who arrived home at an inappropriate moment. A bullet was shot through the rear window of the adulterer's four-wheel drive as he escaped the scene of the crime.

Suddenly, as the bulldozer dragged another track from the car, it jerked and collapsed onto the flat-bed carriage's air-tap (which acts as the brake), damaging it beyond immediate repair and impeding our progress up the line. The fettlers, unperturbed, stood leaning on their picks, but Brass, instantly aware that the mishap could keep us stranded for hours and render the timetable a bigger joke than it already was, uttered obscenities at the gang's incompetence. The engine driver, shaking his head in disgust, clambered

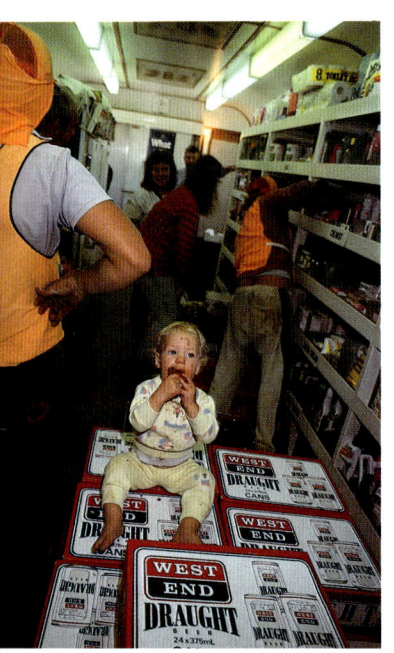

Inside the Tea and Sugar's *unique supermarket van, Joshua Clothier, guards the nectar of the Nullarbor.*

Top *The supermarket manager on the* Tea and Sugar, *Anthony Bothwell, hands long-awaited food supplies to Trevor Whittle, a caretaker of a deserted bomb-testing site, near Watson.* **Above** *On the Nullarbor between Barton and Watson, Bob Copley, guard on the* Tea and Sugar, *hands over to the next guard the traditional ring orders which allow the* Indian Pacific *to proceed.*

Nullarbor wife and mother, Christine Clothier, with son Joshua in the pram, wanders over to the Tea and Sugar *during Watson's fleeting one day of the week visit.*

THE TEA AND SUGAR

from the engine and scaled a steep, sandy embankment beside the track to connect a portable telephone to the wires on the poles to alert Watson, the nearest settlement, to the accident. All that was left for us was to wait for the injured carriage to be towed away by the locomotive to the nearest siding, half an hour away, where it would be dumped for the repairman to worry about. We staggered through the sand and returned to the guard's van.

"I reckon they're just keeping the *Tea and Sugar* going for the wives," Willis said as he searched for the milk as the kettle whistled and rattled on the stove and the *Tea and Sugar* creaked into motion. It seemed an admirable enough criterion to maintain a rail service. "It's a bastard of life out here for them, you know. So far from anything. It's these people's only real association with the outside world."

At last the engine returned, minus the injured carriage, and we were off again down the line and bound for Watson. Not long after, I spotted the fettlers' wives. Christine Clothier was pushing a pram which should have been fitted with four-wheel drive for that rough terrain. She and Alison Matthews were already waiting for the *Tea and Sugar* and waving their weekly shopping lists to greet us. A couple of jovial caretakers from the Maralinga bomb-site, long since closed to interlopers, were there too. The six-year veteran of the retail carriage, Anthony Bothwell—"I'm just a glorified check-out chick, I suppose"—wearing a blue T-shirt and shorts, flung open the door of the van.

"It's the one day of the week," said Alison Matthews, as she made her selections. The baskets, not shelves, were tilted to prevent disasters along the way during those sudden shunts.

"If they ever stopped the *Tea and Sugar*, it really would make life difficult," said Christine Clothier, married to Raymond, an amiable "ganger" or fettler foreman, on the trans-Australian line.

"You'd have to order all your groceries from the supermarket at Port Augusta and have them brought up on freight train. The *Tea and Sugar*'s vital for our morale out here. Sure, it's tough. It'd be a lie if I said I didn't suffer depression. The *Tea and Sugar*'s the social event of the week for us."

Once Christine had finished her shopping she invited me to visit her house. It was made of solid timber, with a huge verandah draped in mosquito netting. She cooked the family meals on a fully operational wood-burning stove—"I even cook pavlovas on that"—to avoid costly electricity bills. Television still hadn't arrived at Watson, but the community had been saving for a satellite dish which they expect will add some relief to their long days.

"We've got no intention of moving at the moment," she said in the lavish shade of the verandah. Watson was having a midsummer "cold snap" with the thermometer reading a coolish 31°C in the late morning. "We like it here. On the Nullarbor you don't hear anything bad and you don't see anything bad. Actually, I like the isolation. I look forward to the *Tea and Sugar*, though every time it leaves you feel like chasing it because there's always some important item you've forgotten to buy. You can't run down the corner shop out here, so you kick yourself and wonder how you could have possibly forgotten anything with a week to think about it."

The excitement was over at Watson and the equilibrium restored for seven days, as the *Tea and Sugar* was in motion again and bound for Cook, the half-way mark and the "big smoke" to the likes of Alison and Christine. Behind us the wives began their afternoon-long task of packing away the booty from the retail van. The routine would resume a week later when the *Tea and Sugar* called again bearing hope and reassurance that the tenacious people of the Nullarbor were not forgotten.

It was time for lunch in the guard's van. During the stop at Watson, Brass had seized some sausages from Anthony in the retail van and they were sizzling in a frypan on the stove, to be accompanied by mashed potato laced with onion. It was the heartiest train meal I had eaten since we left Sydney, though I was stunned to see that Neil was apparently drowning his feast in a murky sun-tan lotion. Worse still, it was sticky, smelly and black.

"Oh, it's black sauce. The wife just rinsed out the sun-cream tube. The sauce bottle kept breaking during the shunts." Between mouthfuls, Brass stared out the window at the desolation again and mumbled.

"Jeez, look at those lush forests, will you? Just look at those beautiful mountains . . ." I told Brass to wake me if he saw any snow-capped peaks and retired to my sleeping berth. I fell asleep as the *Tea and Sugar* squeaked, screeched and crunched along, as all freight trains do with a diverse load, at its leisurely 50 km an hour.

Beside the track at Cook was an oft-quoted sign for visitors which read: "Our hospital needs your help. Get sick. If you're crook come to Cook." A plump young woman strolled past me with a canvas bag of post-office mail over her shoulder and a huge, fierce-looking tattoo just above her elbow. There was a sudden commotion behind me. A young woman hurtled out of the Cook general store, the flyscreen door flapping behind her.

"Hey, Janet!" shouted Dawn, 25 and already a mother of three. "I'm preggers! Just got the results!" Janet smiled feebly, then burst into laughter. "Christ you're a glutton for bloody punishment, aren't you? You're worse than a bloody rabbit, you are!"

Leanne Hancock, a worker at the Cook post office, slings the day's mail destined for the next Indian Pacific, *over her broad shoulders.*

After an exhausting day spent examining the under-belly of trains and enduring the queries of the trans-continentals, train examiner Henry Cox savours his liquid reward.

It seemed to be peak-hour at Cook, roughly the halfway point on the *Tea and Sugar*'s featureless trajectory to Kalgoorlie, the community where we had stopped on the *Indian Pacific* and met the train examiner Henry Cox and his wife, Gloria, a woman so enormous she made the *Indian Pacific* look like a Hornby model. By Nullarbor standards Cook was indeed the big smoke. There was a school, a club-house, a swimming pool and lots of booze. If the independent visitor wants to stay overnight the only accommodation is often a bed in the hospital—the sister-in-charge has sometimes been forced to sleep in the dentist's chair. It is here that in summer, at least, watches are switched back two-and-a-half hours to coincide with Western Australian time.

At Cook the locals aren't allowed to use the retail van, much to their annoyance, because the settlement has its own general store to service the necessities of life which remain, by virtue of the locale, ever frugal. It was the end of the line for us, but not for the *Tea and Sugar*, whose weekly mission remained unfinished with Hughes, Forrest, Rawlinna and Zanthus waiting anxiously up ahead. For us there was the matter of a few hours to wait to hitch the *Trans-Australia*, the Perth-to-Adelaide equivalent of the *Indian Pacific*.

It was heartening, at least, to see that our assessment of Cook coincided with that of the locals, as I relaxed, legs outstretched, enjoying the street theatre from a big rusty railway trolley.

On a rusty railway trolley, outside the general store at Cook on the Nullarbor, a youngster chooses the next best refreshment to the ubiquitous icy ale.

"Not much to do around here, mate," said a smiling man with a little boy. "Except eat, drink, sleep and root." The man disappeared behind the corner of the store, but the little boy, no older than seven or eight, poked his head around and yelled: "Yeah, nothing to do 'cept eat, drink, sleep and root."

On a shady seat outside a house strangled by vines, we waited for 60-year-old Henry Cox, whom we had met the night before. His young, sniffling children were chasing one another around the front yard and in the house we could smell dinner in the oven. On the other side of the town I saw him wiping his brow and emerging from the Cook generator shed. He was on his way home after a hard day's toil.

"Bloody kids," he said, ordering the children indoors to fetch him a beer. "No more for me. I went away and got meself carserated. God-forsaken fuckin' hole, this one. But I reckon it what's you make it, not what it makes you. It's bloody hard work, they get these bloody two-mile-long trains these days and if you're an examiner you've gotta walk 'em. I suppose you're fucking teetotallers coming from Sydney? No? Just as bloody well. I'd shit bricks straight out if I went to Sydney. I'd be frightened of gettin' run over for a start. Port Augusta's getting too big for me. Sydney's a godforsaken fucking sin-hole . . . But I don't class Cook as the bush. No bloody fear. Jeez, this is civilisation next to the places I've been. It's an outer suburb of Port Augusta."

CHAPTER NINE
THE GHAN

It was just as well the original *Ghan* never boasted the prized enticement of its rollicking latter-day counterpart, which revels in its status as the only passenger train on earth fitted with poker machines. The notorious old route from Adelaide to Alice Springs, straight up the spine of Australia via Oodnadatta, could take anywhere between three days and three weeks. The passenger with a passion for one-arm bandits on that long expedition would have been bankrupt by the time he stepped onto the crimson *terra firma* of the so-called Dead Heart. All the mobile gambler of today needs on the contemporary *Ghan* is a dose of luck and five straight Afghan cameljockeys for a jackpot. Since the demise of its predecessor, the modern-day *Ghan* has stripped the journey to just under a day. Yet it is still possible to arrive at the destination with an empty wallet. The moment when the *Ghan* squeezes through Heavitree Gap near The Alice, temptation at last seems to have subsided. But there the passenger discovers a casino beckons seductively from the dry banks of the Todd River.

After an hour or so out of Adelaide the foolhardy fortune-seekers were a picture of concentration as they battled the odds on the pokies inside the "golden wheels" entertainment carriage. The pokies were, in fact, not one-arm bandits, but completely armless. Instead of a lever at the side there was just a button to press. Already, with the journey to Alice Springs still in its infancy, it was obvious that the worst conceivable disaster on this train would not be a derailment but a sudden, debilitating power failure in the pokies car. An American couple were jangling paper coffee cups bulging with silver. The coins were vanishing down the ravenous throat of the machine and, to the Americans' unbridled delight, they multiplied and were regurgitated just as swiftly in the metal tray below.

At Port Augusta Station, the Ghan *is an hour late as agitated passengers await its arrival for the long trek to the Alice.*

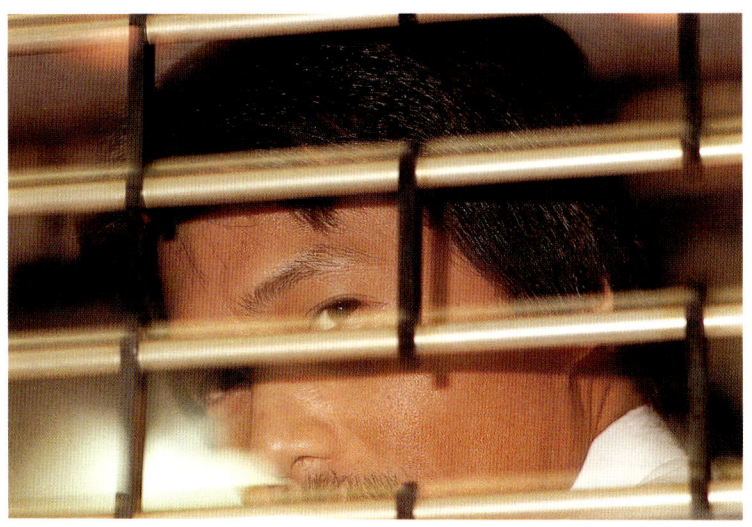

Top *A first-class steward on the* Ghan, *Bernie Luteria, peers through the locked grates of the bar in the Dreamtime Lounge, now closed to imbibers.* **Above** *A convoy of Canadian and American back-packers on the march, as the* Ghan *arrives at Alice Springs Station almost a day after it left Adelaide.*

It was difficult to imagine a better, or for that matter more outlandish, beginning to a rail journey anywhere—even if the maximum pay-out for the pokies was a modest $500, half our return fare, eliminating any chance of an outback sequel to the Great Train Robbery on the edge of the Simpson Desert. If a strip-tease artist had cavorted out of the brake van of the *Ghan* nobody would have been surprised, though I restrained from mentioning it in case an entrepreneurial Australian National Railways adopted it as yet another attraction. Anything, however, was possible on the *Ghan*. If you struck a jackpot you could even treat yourself to a hairdo in the salon in the same entertainment car or select a movie from the video shop and watch it on your personal television set wearing your own headphones. All the details of every service on the train were right there in the thick information kit, *The Ghan— Experiencing the Legend*, that awaited me in my sleeping berth, where I had returned before I too succumbed to the poker machines. "A fully qualified ladies' and men's hairdresser will create a new you for a stylish arrival," it said. It was just a matter of praying that in the event of derailment the hairdresser was at the blow-drying stage of her "creation". The kit was compulsive reading though, packed with useful information.

Each information sheet bore the word "legendary". Legendary Entertainment. Legendary Meals. Legendary Accommodation. But just like on the *Queenslander*, it was the menu that established the ambience and confirmed we were in inhospitable country. In the dining car there was Liechardts (sic) Lust (chicken schnitzel); Jumbuck Special (roast lamb); Rustlers Beef (roast beef); and, yes, Simpson Desert (canned peaches).

"Yeah, aren't those names bloody ridiculous?" said the waiter. "I feel stupid accepting an order for one." I even found a culinary tongue-in-cheek poem in the information kit, written by the head chef of Australian National Railways in a tribute to a colleague called Paddy Greenfield.

Inside the pokies carriage, Brendan Hayes, of Alice Springs, contemplates the likelihood of five straight Afghan camel-jockeys.

*He can knock up a mash
In a lightning-like flash
Or a soup in the wink of an eye
In a minute or two
He'll bash up a stew,
Three minutes to cook up a pie.
All things have a bad side
And I'm sorry to say
That it's true.
He could knock up a custard
In seconds,
But the bloomin' stuff
Tasted like glue!*
(Poem reproduced with kind permission of Australian National Railways.)

The legendary Ghan: *the only train on earth where one moment the passenger can strike a jackpot and the next have her bouffant teased by the resident hairdresser.*

It was as though the *Queenslander*—whose mouth-watering Bundaberg Bombes we had devoured in the excitable company of Arnie the American—was haunting our tracks. On the *Ghan* they were trying as hard to impress as they were on the *Queenslander*, where a well-stocked toiletries kit awaited each first-class traveller. On the *Ghan* I searched everywhere for a toiletries kit, even under the seat, but alas, I was forced to content myself with the information sheets. I had no complaints. The *Queenslander* might have offered a two-piece toothbrush and a tiny tube of paste, but it did not have a poet laureate, nor for that matter, did it have a quiz.

"Question: If there is one 25 cm-wide sleeper placed every 667 mm, how many in a kilometre? Answer: 1,499.25. Question: Now, if there are 1,555 km between Alice Springs and Adelaide, how many sleepers are there overall? Answer: 2,331,334.2. Question: Finally, if each sleeper costs $32 today, what is the cost of laying all those sleepers, not including the labour? Answer: $74,602,694.40."

I suspected the last question had been cleverly inserted in the event that the Federal Minister for Transport should board the *Ghan* one day, read it, and be so moved, he would return to Canberra vowing to rescue the railways from financial damnation. I appreciated the information in the brochure. Now I was armed with crucial data that any self-respecting rail-buff would kill to have in his notebook. The *Ghan*'s name, by the way, was inspired by the Afghan camel drivers and their beasts, who formed the chief transport link from Alice to the Red Centre in the 1860s.

Inevitably, I was drawn back to the fascination of the entertainment car where the poker machine was still spewing coins at the Americans, the female half of whom was just as intently shoving the coins back down the slot with a scowl that was most inappropriate, seeing that she had just deprived Australian National Railways of considerable revenue.

"Honey," he said. "One day, you never know, you might have your *own* money to put into the slot machines." The husband, who had never introduced himself or offered me the opportunity to do likewise, looked around as though for reassurance that he was recognised as the bread-winner and that was *his* money down the pokies' metallic gullets. His wife seemed conditioned to his strategic humiliations. A Swedish couple, who had no interest in playing the pokies, had joined us in the entertainment car, out of curiosity.

"Say, what do those coo-coo-burr-rers look like?" he asked the Swedes, ignoring the fact that I, a native Australian like the bird, might have an answer. The Swedes didn't have a clue, so I volunteered a description of one, even demonstrating its laugh. The American, who wore a blue, white and red T-

Half-way around the world, on an outback train, Canadians Cherie Nash and John Huzil, strangers until now, discover unexpected romance across the aisle of the Ghan.

shirt with "Australia" written on it, seemed oddly dissatisfied by my description. I suspected that he suspected, for reasons unknown to this day, that I was lying and attempting to embarrass him in front of the Swedes.

The American ignored us all again and thumped his wife on the back, her scowl ever-lengthening as she slipped another coin in the machine which returned half a cupful of silver. He was exhilarated by the sight of salt-flats, not much bigger than ponds, on either side of the *Ghan*. I had battled the rail-buffs; now I found myself in the presence of a committed salt-flat fanatic. I could have walked away, I suppose, but I decided to stay and document a heretofore undocumented species. The Swedes were as mystified as I was at the American's fascination. The salt-lakes were merely the size of ponds and I feared for his state of mind when he witnessed their bigger counterparts nearer Alice Springs.

"Hey, look at this," he said, frantically alternating between each side of the carriage. "It's amazing. I never seen salt-pans like that in my *entire* life. Isn't that just amazing? I just love the outback. Just look at it!"

At this point relations between myself and the American suddenly deteriorated to the stage where I would never be invited to look him up next time I was in Atlanta, Georgia.

"I'm afraid that technically," I said good-humouredly, "what you see out there is not *really* the outback. We've only just left Adelaide." The *Ghan*, after all, was just an hour or so out of the city, which according to my information kit was once described by *New Yorker* magazine as "possibly the last well-planned, well-governed and moderately-contented metropolis on earth." The

A passenger on the Ghan *enjoying a light literary stimulant.*

hills were still undulating and the locals beside the track still wore designer labels. The American, however, would have none of it.

"Yeah?" he growled, his face a soft shade of red. "Well, it sure as hell looks like the outback to me, fella!" The Swedes winced. They recognised this sort of outburst from tennis matches between Bjorn Borg and John McEnroe. I left the entertainment car before I felt compelled to correct the American on any further cultural nuances and sought the sanctuary of my berth to read the next chapter of the information kit and pray that the American and I were not allotted the same table at dinner.

Since 6 August 1929, when the first train arrived at Alice Springs, the *Ghan* has serviced the line between Adelaide and Alice Springs. The old route was prone to flooding and plagues of termites dined regularly on the sleepers, making the journey unreliable and hazardous if the traveller's itinerary was not elastic. On one occasion the old *Ghan* was stranded by a flood for two weeks and when the reserves of food were exhausted, the engineman was forced to shoot the goats on board to placate his passengers' hunger. Before the new line along more reliable terrain was opened on 26 November 1980, the old *Ghan* ran on the primitive route. Now, just outside Alice Springs, the *Ghan* Preservation Society has restored a section of the old *Ghan* rail line and restored some old carriages and locomotives. A section of the Overland Telegraph Line between Adelaide and Darwin, which was completed by Sir Charles Todd in 1872 (an engineering feat in its day), has also been resuscitated. On 5 October 1985, 30 km of the old railway line, the work of committed locals, was re-opened. The Iron Man statue, built from scrap pieces of railway track, stands at the northbound 1,390 km point, a commemoration by railway workers of the one-millionth concrete sleeper between Tarcoola to the south and Alice Springs to the north.

After dinner—where I had succumbed to the Straight From The Heart soup, the Simpson Desert dessert and, of course, the "Liechardts" Lust chicken—I retired to the Dreamtime Lounge Car where alcohol was lubricating cautious conversation. It was becoming dark and the *Ghan* was God-knows where. A fiery red ribbon had formed on the horizon as the sun slid slowly out of sight. Outside the terrain was undergoing a silent transformation that would not reveal itself as desert until dawn. All the window offered us were our own reflections from the fluorescent lights of the lounge car. An Englishman lifted the lid of the piano, a real one this time, and tinkled a melody in a futile attempt to inspire a sing-along. A few of the Swedes mumbled words to a song they did not know and the Englishman gave up and returned to his whisky-and-dry.

In the Dreamtime Lounge Car I met Butch, a retired Tasmanian miner who had abandoned the frigid Apple Isle in favour of the hot Dead Heart of the mainland. He had travelled inland from Queenstown to catch an overnight ferry across Bass Strait to Melbourne. From there he boarded the *Overland* train to Adelaide; and from there he had made it to the lounge car of the legendary *Ghan* to down an ale in exceptional spirits. Beside him was an expatriate New Zealander from Sydney called Richard, a balding former cab-driver with a law degree, who was bound for Alice Springs to meet his wife, a doctor whose main task was to care for the mission Aborigines. A young Italian girl from Mildura was animated on a lounge beside the piano, chatting with a couple of young men, who were brothers. The extrovert one had just graduated from law school and was on his way to Indonesia via Darwin, while the subdued one, his face buried for most of the trip in a medical dictionary, was destined for Darwin where he had accepted an internship at a local hospital. At Alice Springs the Italian girl would begin her career as a teacher at a local Catholic school. Robert, a born-again Christian from Perth, had a beer in his hand instead of a Good News Bible, which he had left in his compartment. His car, which he intended to drive from Alice Springs to Darwin, was riding piggy-back on the train. I produced a couple of bottles of champagne that had been left in my berth by Australian National and poured a glass for each of them. It was the happiest night of the trip and I raised a private toast to the manifest differences in personality, philosophy and purpose that separated us and drank another to the special train that had united us all. The Swedish contingent on the *Ghan*, smiling demurely at the extrovert Australians, were a terrible disappointment. Not one of them even

Top *The rigours of economy travel on the* Ghan.   **Above** *A highlight of the* Ghan *trip— a spectacular sunset outside Port Augusta.*

Above *A hungry and sleepy Rebecca Noble materialises for breakfast on the* Ghan.
Right *Inside the dining car, a Swedish passenger awaits her serving of "Liechardt's Lust".*

THE GHAN

remotely resembled Stefan Edberg, but their manners were as impeccable as any of their racket-wielding compatriots. The John McEnroe of the pokies van had gone to bed, probably counting Afghan camel-jockeys to get to sleep.

The next morning the *Ghan* passed above the Finke River across the largest bridge on the Adelaide to Alice Springs line. Although usually dry the Finke had become a shallow creek lapping at an ever-broadening sandy bed. In the infrequent periods of heavy rains it could become a raging torrent. The route map in the *Ghan* information kit told me that legend had the Finke as the oldest river in the world. The Simpson Desert begins just north of the river. An hour or so later we passed Pine Gap, the mysterious joint Australian-American defence facility, its domed roofs poking out of the red earth like scoops of vanilla ice-cream. In the far distance I could see the pass through ranges, Heavitree Gap. The *Ghan* squeezed through the huge canyons, past an Aboriginal camp where the train is often forced to stop for bodies on the line. A week or so before our arrival the train had actually passed over a drunken Aboriginal woman lying there, flagon at her side. It was only her extreme thinness, so they say, which saved her from an ugly death under the wheels of the *Ghan*. At midday it was 40°C in Alice Springs. All the romance of the Dead Heart had been sapped by the terrors of tourism. The main street was a mall where there were shopping complexes and automatic teller machines, and I abandoned all faith when I learned that there was a multi-storey Sheraton beside the Todd River. But it was too hot for sight-seeing and I regretfully succumbed to the coolness of the Sheraton to watch the cricket on television in the bar and wait for the return journey later that afternoon.

Back on the train the disaster I had forecast had occurred. The electricity supply to the pokies car—and indeed the entire train—had failed in the heat. The passengers had been ordered to close the shutters on all the *Ghan*'s venetian blinds to prevent the engine's powerhouse from overheating. There was little else to do except sit in my berth and wait for the Afghan camel-jockeys to start twirling for some lucky fortune-seeker again. I increased the volume on the radio. The fanfare for the ABC news filled the cabin. My ears twitched at the second story about the local dog-catcher. Despite great risk he had, the announcer revealed, acted with great valour and humanity in the capture of an unlicensed stray mongrel in the car-park of a local bank. The bank manager, who had seen it all, was moved to nominate the dog-catcher for a commendation at the next meeting of council. The laurel was approved and the alderman announced at the next meeting that this humble collector of homeless canines was "the finest dog-catcher that Alice Springs had seen for many, many years". The lights flickered on again, an icy breeze from the air-conditioning surged through the *Ghan* and it was feeding-time again in the pokies van.

(123)

CHAPTER TEN
THE BLUE LAKE, THE INTER-CITY DAYLINK, THE SUNRAYSIA, THE SILVER CITY COMET, AND THE XPT

High above the city to the east, the Adelaide Hills sat above the flat urban expanse like giant khaki Akubra hats, but their serenity concealed the danger in the scrub. When the trains crawl around the twisting, lofty terraces and probe in and out of the tunnels in search of the open riverland on the distant other side, the threat comes not from bush-fires, nor the odd fallen tree-trunk on the tracks, nor even the steep incline itself. It is the rogue millipedes that cause alarm. At their most pernicious, they march out of the bush and ride the rails. When an unsuspecting loco chugs up the line the millipedes it minces turn the track into a slippery slide. Sometimes a locomotive has to wait at the bottom of the hills to push trains that lose their traction this way. The perilous millipedes, however, were inconspicuous the day the *Blue Lake* (just two carriages and an array of empty seats) left the hills behind for Mount Gambier and hurtled downhill on a giant embankment that would take us inland, down the narrow strip between South Australia and the border of Victoria—and safely out of millipede territory. For the first time since we left the starkly modern Adelaide Rail Terminal, the *Blue Lake* could at last summon back its puff. There was no dining car and, by the look of it, no company worth cultivating.

After scaling the Adelaide Hills at the speed of a millipede, the Mount Gambier-bound Blue Lake *comparatively rockets down the other side.*

(124)

Top left *A vigil on the* Blue Lake *as night falls across golden wheatfields which fan either side of the track.* **Top right** *The elusive* Blue Lake *6.30 pm chicken arriving at 7.25 pm.* **Above** *A packed economy-class carriage on the* Inter-city Daylink *from Warrnambool to Melbourne, a swift three-hour jaunt across the state.*

THE BLUE LAKE

The serenity of the *Blue Lake*, which derives its name from a cobalt expanse of water of the same name at Mount Gambier, offered me a moment for reflection. It was almost a month and a half since the *Pacific Coast Motorail* left Central Station at the beginning of our quest to traverse Australia by train. For the first time since we left Sydney, I felt as though I was homeward bound. But I had deluded myself. First, the *Blue Lake* would have to reach Mount Gambier; then there was a bus to catch to Warrnambool where the swift *Inter-city Daylink* would be waiting to take us to Melbourne; the *Sunraysia* would convey us to Mildura; then we would go by road in a hired vehicle to Broken Hill to keep our appointment with the gloriously named *Silver City Comet*; finally, we would journey on the sleek *XPT* from Orange to Sydney. I balanced my head against the icy window in a mild state of depression. At Central Station I had started the journey in search of people, but now I found myself seeking ways to avoid them. Not unlike a slow-acting drug, the contorted Australian railway network, marvel though it may be with its lines that suddenly end in the middle of nowhere, had rendered me a virtual misanthrope. For a second or two I wondered if it was the sound of *Tea For Two* on the electronic hands-free organ of the *Indian Pacific* that still reverberated inside my head. All I knew was that I wanted to hand in my badge as a trainee rail-buff and fly, like every other sane being in the country with enough money to spend. I sank into the vinyl seat and pulled the shutter down in case a jet should screech overhead on its way to Sydney and I would wish I was on it.

Yet as I sat there, the gentle rocking motion of the train, as ever, rocked me out of my neurosis. It was at least reassuring to have passed through wooded country after our wanderings around the Nullarbor and the Simpson Desert aboard the *Indian Pacific*, the *Tea and Sugar* and the *Ghan*. The steward on the *Blue Lake*, who had removed his bow-tie now that we were out of sight of officialdom, asked if I would be interested in the 6.30 pm chicken. I nodded and handed over my money. But the *Blue Lake* was running late. The 6.30 pm chicken became the 6.45 pm chicken, then the 7 pm chicken and then the 7.15 pm chicken until finally the train stopped and the steward (by now a stewardess to be sure who had boarded for the next shift) heaved a steaming box full of dinners into the brake van. The 6.30 pm chicken had arrived but it was now the 7.25 pm chicken. The 6.30 pm chicken is all I recall of our trip on the *Blue Lake*. Oh, and the killer millipedes.

The next day we caught a bus from Mount Gambier to Warrnambool where we had arranged to make our next rail connection through the immense pine plantations beside the road, across the border and along the coastline. Here Irish immigrants had settled and transformed the temperate, wild coastal country, which sharply resembled their homeland, into their own

At Geelong, Margaret disembarks from the Daylink, *armed with a trio of grandchildren, a half-eaten packet of Teddy Bear biscuits and on a search for a $25 Japanese ornament made in South Korea.*

THE INTER-CITY DAYLINK

breath of fresh Eire. The Irish heritage survives intact. At Port Fairy, a delightful historical enclave, the houses were stolid, stone affairs tiny enough in such a vast corner of the world to be an architectural Irish joke. At seaside Warrnambool the cool breeze that blew from Bass Strait gently rustled the sprightly Norfolk pines which lined the streets. The orange bus stopped outside the railway station, which resembled a sanitarium—and indeed, it was madness as the travellers bade their long farewells to loved ones on the platform. It occurred to me that I had ignored the art of the railway farewell during our journey. I had noticed them, sure enough, but it was not until here at Warrnambool that I savoured their significance. At the airport there is time for a hug and a kiss, but before you know it loved ones have vanished behind a partition to be frisked with a metal detector and then sucked into a cold, thin tube. At the railway station the platform offers all sorts of chances to linger until the exact last moment when the train pulls away, and there they still are with noses squashed against the window, waving one frantic last goodbye as you chase the train down the track a little way.

On the *Inter-city Daylink* from Warrnambool to Melbourne, the bearded Tasmanian-bound Canadian, were it not for the shortness of his stature, might have been a caricature of a lumberjack. Besides, inside his bag there was not an axe or a checked jacket, but lurid magazines. He caught me glancing at the contents of his open suitcase as he peeked over the cover of *Sex Jokes*, full of crude cartoons of buxom secretaries seated on the laps of gleeful bosses mouthing saucy one-liners. Yet he was so earnest that he didn't laugh even once at jokes. His absence of laughter caused me to suspect that maybe the Canadian was concealing a copy of Joyce's *Ulysses* in the fold of *Sex Jokes*, in case it provoked the anger of the anti-intellectuals in economy. I recalled how we used to sit in class at school with our biology text-books held high enough to hide the illicit copy of *Grunt* in which ecstatic women performed all sorts of lithe sexual acrobatics. When he finished *Sex Jokes* he rifled his bag and pulled out another magazine. It was *More Sex Jokes*, and was obviously no wittier than its moribund predecessor. He did not giggle at any of the cartoons in that one either, though *More Sex Jokes* took a slightly different tack. It had fewer cartoons about secretaries and bosses and was more devoted to dirty old men. He offered me *Sex Jokes*, to keep if I wished. The *Inter-city Daylink* veered inland and hurtled across the heartland of Victoria as I waited for the Canadian to produce his copy of *Yet More Sex Jokes*.

Although we had left the cyclones behind weeks ago in Queensland, I watched as a typhoon blew through the carriage—a woman in her late 50s. She wore spectacles with exaggerated rims that curled at the edges near the temples, like the models which adorn Dame Edna Everage. Her lipstick was smeared over the edges like a young child's colouring-in. She had boarded

TICKET TO RIDE

the *Daylink* at a nondescript little town called Colac with a portable crèche in tow, blocking the aisle in economy with a pram containing one of three grandchildren. She was armed with a crumpled packet of Teddy Bear biscuits in case the children became restless, though she confessed that she had already eaten half of them herself back on the platform. She plumped down next to me and introduced herself as Margaret. The Canadian put aside his copy of *More Sex Jokes* and for the first time a smile creased his face. Her destination was Geelong, a few hours down the line, where she intended to buy for the family mantelpiece another $25 fake Japanese ornament made in South Korea—a mounted piece of carved plywood in the shape of a Shinto temple bathed in splintered cherry blossoms. She showed me the one she had in her bag.

"I rang the lady at the shop before I left," she confided. "She told me there was only one left and that I'd better hurry. I just hope that I get there in time. Isn't it beautiful? Those Asians are so clever." But her new South Korean "Japanese" artifact would have to be her last. The money wasn't coming into the household since her husband went onto workers' compensation. "He's had brain surgery, you know," she said. "A clot or something, they said. He's been off for four weeks and he's still not back at work. We haven't been dancing for months. He's hopeless." I could scarcely believe what I had heard. It was only an hour ago that I had seen a wobbly figure farewelling her at Colac with a walking-stick. One of her grandchildren, who appeared as mystified by his grandmother as I had become during our brief but informative association, began to cry. Unfazed, Margaret stuffed a Teddy Bear biscuit in its mouth, had one herself and related the harrowing story of her daughter's divorce.

A day later on Platform Five at Melbourne's Spencer Street Station, a grim place which would have resembled a mausoleum were it not for a huge mural of trains, I noticed that all those stories about Elvis Presley still being alive were true after all. He was standing on the platform with his landlady, waiting for the *Sunraysia* to Mildura where he headed for his annual stint as a grape-picker. An over-sized red comb poked out of the pocket of his tight black trousers which co-ordinated with a black shirt emblazoned with silver studs. His black hair was slicked back with some excess of lubricant. He wore reflective sunglasses and a precisely shaven moustache. The moustache gave him away. It wasn't Elvis at all. He introduced himself as plain old Nick Pappas, a tip-truck driver from Sunshine. Besides, Elvis would never have allowed his landlady to wave him off at the railway station. When the vines ripen in February each year, the line up to Mildura through the arid Mallee country and beyond to the border of New South Wales is full of trains stacked with opportunists seeking the fast money of fruit-picking season. The

Right *On the* Sunraysia, *Francis Goldie Mau, former Tongan Rugby Union team vice-captain, awakens after an afternoon nap.* **Bottom right** *Upon arrival at St Arnaud, the journey at least for some, is at its end . . .*

On his annual pilgrimage to Mildura for the grape-picking season, Nick Pappas, Elvis Presley devotee, heads north on his holidays to escape the tedium of a city existence.

overnight trip could be an experience in itself. A few of the other pickers on board the *Sunraysia*, heading for Mildura before all the cheap accommodation was snapped up by others, told of the women who service the men for $20 each on the trip to Mildura. The journey on the *Sunraysia* had become an annual pilgrimage for the likes of Nick Pappas, too.

"I go for the country life, the sunshine and the fresh air which is something different to Melbourne," said Pappas. "The money doesn't come into it for me. You get all sorts. Aborigines, Italians, Maltese, Fijians and Greeks. They all pile up. I'm on holidays at the moment, but I'd get too bored, so I spend my six weeks up here."

Beside the track, as the *Sunraysia* rolled on somewhere towards Mildura, big-busted old women in crisp white uniforms, bowled big brown balls down well-watered rinks as they clutched umbrellas for protection from the sun.

At Mildura there was no time to linger over the beauty of ripe vines. The line ended at the border and there was the matter of the two-and-a-half-hour drive north straight up the curveless road to Broken Hill for our final swoop on Sydney. A woman from the hire-car company jangled the keys of a four-wheel drive and warned us to be off the road before sunset, when kangaroos would swarm over the road. The rental contract was grimly stamped: "No insurance for cars damaged by kangaroos". But we survived and so did the roos.

The skyline of Broken Hill, all wires, furnaces and dirt mounds, reared above the horizon. Although I had never visited Broken Hill I had seen its commercial television station in South Australia. I remembered that it was quite possibly the worst I had ever seen. Many of the commercials appeared to be read from crudely handwritten messages on bits of coloured card. I fell asleep in the poky motel room watching an ABC documentary on the history of surgery just as the narrator was salivating over the miracles of brain operations in nauseating detail.

The *Silver City Comet* must be one of the most inaccurately named trains in the world. It is, in reality, less like a comet and more like the spark of a roman candle. The trip between Broken Hill would take a full half day and then there was a five-hour trip ahead of us on the *XPT*. The *Comet*, in peeling silver with a light blue stripe, had left Broken Hill at 4.10 am, surely one of the earliest departure times for any passenger train in Australia if not the free world. Everything that I laughed off at the beginning, all the little quirks and minor irritations, now left me in a state of almost intractable irritability. But it

A lightning early-morning stop for the Silver City Comet *at Menindee, an hour or so east of Broken Hill, yet less than an agonising dozen hours to Orange.*

TICKET TO RIDE

was 4.30 am before the train left the platform. Through one eye, the other one still asleep, I watched the sun heave above the horizon like a furnace of orange and red with a smoky blue fringe. Trains always offer the best viewpoint to watch the majesty of a sunrise. The day unravelled just as the track unravelled. It would be wrong to say I was unimpressed, but by now I had seen too many sunrises, and had risen too early to catch too many trains, with too many towns left undiscovered, because we had arrived in the night and were gone by the morning.

Once it was fully illuminated and I was conscious enough, I could see it was an antique of a train—reminiscent of the *Dirranbandi Mail* but devoid of its charm. If it had been six weeks before and the beginning of our journey, I might have been more enchanted by the *Silver City Comet*. At each end of the wood-panelled carriage there were old black and white photographs of New South Wales scenes. The *Comet* had an unscheduled appointment with the railyards where it would be dumped to die like many other New South Wales trains withdrawn from service because of cost inefficiencies. Any train that forced its passengers to rise so early, I decided bitterly, deserved to be retired. Although the train was a museum piece that had just celebrated its first half-century, air-conditioning had been fitted, but it was so cold I huddled into the corner of my seat for warmth. I knew the father in front of me worked on the railways when he threatened to lock his young son in the brake van if he continued to misbehave. I allowed my sausage roll, which I had bought from a cantankerous old person in the dining-car, to freeze beside me and dozed off in an attempt to forget the hours ahead to Orange.

No less important because of its antiquity, the sign at Boremore Station.

At Orange, getting off the *Silver City Comet* and onto the *XPT* was like entering a time-tunnel. Not that the *XPT* was all that state-of-the-art. When it was commissioned it was billed as the fastest train in the land and hailed as the sleek saviour of the deeply troubled New South Wales railways. But someone must have stuck something in the trumpet when the fanfare was played because it still took five hours to Sydney. Outside, its black, red and orange colour scheme and the shape of the nose on the engine suggested sleekness, but the inside was bilious in all shades of orange.

On every train, no matter how comfortable, cheerful, or efficient, there was always at least one fellow passenger to inject a shot of intolerance through your veins. Here it was a frail old woman with the most deathly cough I had ever heard, a cough that threatened to rip open her chest at each spasm. She seemed to suffer the fearful delusion that the cigarettes she smoked were in some way therapeutic. Wheeze, cough, splutter. Wheeze, cough, splutter. Wheeze, cough, splutter. When she returned from the food bar in the next carriage she complained to her husband that she was out of breath and she lit up another cigarette. Wheeze, cough, splutter. There was no

At the controls of the Silver City Comet, *engineman Graeme Vale, thrusts the train eastwards, across the breadth of New South Wales, as the first rays of sun drench his cabin.*

The twin strands of steel that guided us northwards, a month and a half ago, now beckon us back, as the train rolls inexorably eastwards towards Sydney and home.

escape. And so it went for five hours. If ever the anti-smoking movement had wished for the ultimate deterrent, it was to be found in a smoke-filled first-class cabin on the *XPT*. Wheeze, cough, splutter. Wheeze, cough, splutter. Wheeze, cough, splutter. For one hideous moment I nodded off and dreamt the train was a cancer ward.

The silver streak of the train curled cautiously around the lush cliffs of the Blue Mountains, defying the sheer drops to the valleys below. It dashed in and out of tunnels, skirting the incline and squeezing through narrow cuttings. It was near sunset when the train twisted around a corner and I glimpsed a magnificent view. A chain of mountains, in the sun's weakening light, receded into the distance like a delicate Chinese painting. An hour out of Sydney, in the company of a Dane, his Australian girlfriend and an Englishman, we cracked open cans of beer in a rowdy, impromptu celebration. I suppose I was too dazed to propose a toast to a journey that in its planning seemed absurd, in its execution preposterous, and now—almost 20,000 km later, at the end of the line—an act of insanity.

"Around Australia by train?" the incredulous had asked. "But no one catches trains any more!" I cupped my hands over the reflective sheen on the window and saw that we were edging towards the loveliness of the old sandstone clock-tower of Central Station, floodlit and boldly announcing that we had made it. I wondered if the Mussolini in blue railway shorts was still bleating in the luggage office, but I was far too weary to investigate. I remembered, as I staggered off the train, that we had left Central Station with that thick wad of tickets almost a month and a half ago to the day. Now just one ticket remained—the one for the *XPT*—and I tore it up and dropped it into a bin. It was a gesture of finality and, most important, one of achievement. The auditors were probably still locked away in their dimly lit offices, plotting to send another train to its doom. But we had beaten them before they could wield their pencils and decree that another line be closed. Slowly, I trod back into a stationary reality with half my body still on a train somewhere down a distant line.

APPENDIX — RAIL INFORMATION

NEW SOUTH WALES
The Pacific Coast Motorail
Route: Sydney to Murwillumbah. Introduced: 1973 (as the Gold Coast Motorail). Distance: 935 kilometres. Duration of Journey: 17 hours. Frequency: daily. Engine Type: 86 class to Broadmeadow, then 442 type engine to Murwillumbah. Gauge: standard.

The Silver City Comet
Route: Broken Hill to Orange. Introduced: 1937. Distance: 1,125 kilometres. Duration of journey: 12 hours. Frequency: thrice weekly. Engine type: diesel. Gauge: standard.

The Central West XPT
Route: Orange to Sydney. Introduced: 1982. Distance: 323 kilometres. Duration of journey: four hours. Frequency: daily. Engine type: diesel. Gauge: standard.

QUEENSLAND
Dirranbandi Mail
Route: Brisbane to Dirranbandi. Introduced: 1913. Distance: 668 kilometres. Duration of journey: 19 hours. Frequency: twice weekly. Engine type: diesel electric locomotive; predominantly built by Clyde Engineering, Brisbane; mostly commissioned following demise of steam in late 1960s. Gauge: narrow.

Westlander
Route: Cunnamulla to Charleville. Introduced: 1954. Distance: 972 kilometres (Brisbane to Cunnamulla). Duration of journey: 21 hours. Frequency: twice weekly each way. Engine type: diesel electric. Gauge: narrow.

Midlander
Route: Winton to Rockhampton. Introduced: 1954. Distance: 863 kilometres. Duration of journey: 19 hours. Frequency: twice weekly each way. Engine type: diesel electric. Gauge: narrow.

Queenslander
Route: Brisbane to Cairns. Introduced: 1986. Distance: 1681 kilometres. Duration of journey: 32 hours. Frequency: weekly each way. Engine type: diesel electric. Gauge: narrow.

Gulflander
Route: Normanton to Croydon. Introduced: 1891. Distance: 152 kilometres. Duration of journey: four hours. Frequency: weekly to Croydon return. Engine type: during our visit DL diesel mechanical locomotive; four built for Queensland railways for the Forsyth line, but normally a pre-Second World War rail motor; former inspector's car out of Rockhampton, commissioned for Gulflander mid-1984. Gauge: narrow.

SOUTH AUSTRALIA AND WESTERN AUSTRALIA
The Ghan
Route: Alice Springs (Northern Territory) to Adelaide. Introduced: 1980. Distance: 1,336 kilometres. Duration of journey: 22 hours. Frequency: twice weekly each way (present-day Ghan). Engine type: diesel electric usually GM class. Gauge: standard.

Indian Pacific
Route: Perth to Sydney. Introduced: 1970. Distance: 3,961 kilometres. Duration of journey: 65 hours. Frequency: three times weekly each way. Engine type: diesel electric between Perth and Lithgow in the Blue Mountains of NSW. At Lithgow electric locomotives are attached for the run to Sydney. Gauge: standard throughout.

Tea and Sugar
Route: Port Augusta to Kalgoorlie. Introduced: 1917. Distance: 1,689 kilometres. Duration of journey: three days. Frequency: weekly. Engine type: diesel electric locomotives. Gauge: standard.

The Blue Lake
Route: Adelaide to Mount Gambier. Introduced: 1984. Distance: 490 kilometres. Duration of journey: six and a half hours. Frequency: six days. Engine type: rail car.

The Mount Newman Mining iron ore train
Route: Port Hedland to Newman. Introduced: 1969. Distance: 426 kilometres. Duration of journey: eight hours. Frequency: six times daily. Engine type: General Electric 7/8 and Alco diesel locomotives. Gauge: standard.

VICTORIA

Daylink between Warrnambool and Melbourne
Route: Warrnambool to Melbourne. Introduced: 1980. Distance: 267 kilometres. Duration of journey: four hours. Frequency: three times a day. Engine type: N-class 2400 HP. Gauge: 5'3".

The Sunraysia
Route: Melbourne to Mildura. Introduced: 1987. Distance: 566 kilometres. Duration of journey: 9 hours and 10 minutes (northbound). Frequency: thrice weekly. Engine type: N-class 2400 HP. Gauge: 5'3".

APPENDIX—PHOTOGRAPHIC INFORMATION

As fantastic was the prospect of taking the photographs for *Ticket to Ride*, there were many problems associated with the assignment.

Endeavouring to be as candid as possible, I decided to "shoot" as many available light situations as I could. Lumbering around from carriage to carriage with Nikons and Metz flashes around my neck would soon give the game away. Hence the most used lens for my internal shots was a Nikkor 135 mm F2. I used 200 ASA Kodachrome film generally exposed at between 1/30th sec to 1/125th sec at F2. The other lens that came in for a hiding was the Nikkor 35 mm F2, using Kodachrome 64 ASA at exposures between 1/8th sec to 1/60th sec at F2. The two cameras that I used were Nikon F3 H.P.s. It was pointless using tripods as the trains, especially on the narrow Queensland gauge, were lurching around at alarming degrees. I braced myself as best I could, being very steady with the shutter finger and then waited for the right moment.

Another problem was how to get exterior shots of the trains I was travelling on. There was nothing more frustrating than speeding across the Nullarbor with an absolutely fantastic sunset dropping over the flat plain only to view it through double glazing with condensation forming between the two panes. So whenever or wherever a train would stop, I would leap out, quickly reconnoitre picture possibilities, work out camera angles, and shoot. In one instance, in the middle of the Nullarbor, the *Indian Pacific* started to pull away after a two minute stop, not realising that I had hopped off the train and was obscured from the driver's view by a rock (pages 90–91). With two Nikons swinging wildly around my neck I only just managed to get back on board before the loco had built up too much speed. But great photographic assignments are made all the more enjoyable by overcoming certain obstacles, and I hope that you find our venture around Australia as exciting and enjoyable as we both did.

I N D E X

Adelaide, SA   101, 113, 118, 119, 123, 124
Alice Springs, NT   113, (114), 117, 119, 120, 123
Alpha, Qld   42, 45
Arnie the American   46, 48, 51, 52, (53), 55

Babinda, Qld   (50)
Bass Strait   120, 129
Blackbull, Qld   64
Blue Lake   124, (125), (126)
Blue Mountains, NSW   140
Bothwell, Anthony   (105), 107, 108
Brisbane, Qld   (18), 20, (21), 22, 27, (28-29), 30, 35, 39, 57
Broken Hill, NSW   12, 127, 133

Cairns, Qld   22, 36, 46, (54-55), 59
Casino, NSW   14
Central Station, Sydney   (10), 11, 12, (12), 127, 140
Charleville, Qld   36, 39
Chichester Ranges, WA   77
Clews, Jeff   42, 43
Clothier, Christine   (106), 107, 108
Clothier, Raymond   107
Cocks, Barry   35, 36, (37)
Colac, Vic   129, 130
Cook, SA   97, 108, 110, 111
Cooper, Jamie   (70)
Cox, Gloria   110
Cox, Henry   97, (110), 110, 111
Croydon, Qld   57, 59, 63
Cummings, Greg   64, (66), 67, (68), (69)
Cunnamulla, Qld   35, 36

Darwin, NT   67, 119, 120
Derby, WA   73, 74, 76
Dirranbandi, Qld   22, 27, 30, 33, 35, 36
Dirranbandi Mail   20, (21), 22, (23), (24), (25), (26), 27, (27), 30, (31), (32), 33, 35, 39
Donkin, Tom   79
Douglas family   (65)

Fettlers   104
Finke River, NT   123
Fitzroy Crossing, WA   70, 73, 74
Forrest, WA   110

Ghan   12, 113, (114), 115, (115), (116), 117, 118, (118), 119, (119), 120, (121), (122), 123, 127
Goondiwindi, Qld   33
Greenfield, Paddy   115
Gulflander   12, 57, 59, (60), (61), (62), 63, 64
Gulf of Carpentaria   12, 57, 63, 64, 67

Hamilton, Neil   103, 108
Hancock, Leanne   (108-109)
Hawke, Bob   91, 93
Hayes, Brendan   (115)
Heavitree Gap, NT   113, 123
Hughenden, Qld   59
Hughes, WA   110

International Express   12
Indian Pacific   12, 51, 84, (84), (86), 87, 88, (89), 90, (90), 91, 93, 94, (96), 97, 98, 99, 110, 127
Iron Ore Train   12, 73, (75), 76, 77, (76-77), 79, (80-81)
Inter-city Daylink   127, (128), 129

Kalgoorlie, WA   85, (86), 87, (87), (94), (95), 100
Kay, Dick   (70), (72)
Kubill Siding, Qld   (35)
Kununurra, WA   70

Lane, Don   48
Longreach, Qld   (40), (41), 42
Luteria, Bernie   (114)

Mackay, Qld   52
Maralinga, SA   107
Marble Bar, WA   77
Matthews, Alison   107, 108
Mau, Francis Goldie   (131)
McPherson, Ken   33
Melbourne, Vic   129, 130, 133
Menindee, NSW   (134-135)
Menk, Dick   (44), 45
Midlander   36, 42, (44), 45, 48
Mildura, Vic   127, 130, 133
Mount Gambier, SA   124, 127
Mount Isa, Qld   56, 64, 67, 69
Mount Whaleback, WA   77
Murwillumbah, NSW   14

Newman, WA   12, 76, 77
Noack, Reverend   103
Noble, Rebecca   (122)
Normanton, Qld   (56), 57, 59, 63, 64, 67
Nullarbor Plain   12, 87, 94, 97, 98, 100, 101, 103, 104, 107, 108, 110, 111
Nurina, WA   94

O'Neill, David   76, (76), 79, 83
Oodnadatta, SA   113
Ooldea, WA   94
Orange, NSW   127, 136

Pacific Coast Motorail   12, 14, 15, (15), (16-17), 19, 35, 124
Pappas, Nick   130, (132), 133

Perth, WA   83, 90, 91, 101
Phillips, George   63
Pilbara, WA   76, 79
Pine Gap, NT   123
Port Augusta, SA   100, 111, (112)
Port Fairy, Vic   127
Port Hedland, WA   12, 67, 73, 76

Queenslander   12, 22, 36, 46, 48, (48), (49), (50), 51, (51), 52, (53), 54, 55, (54-55), 93, 117
Quirk, Tanya   64

Rail-buff   22, (24-25), 27, 30, 33, 52, 54, 55, 93
Rawlinna, WA   110
Redmont, WA   77, 79, (79), 83
Reich, Charles   22, (24-25), 27, 30, 33
Robertson, Clive   5
Rockhampton, Qld   36, 42, 45, (47)
Roma Street Station, Brisbane   20, 30, 33, 48

Satoshi and Takashi   87, 88, (92), 93
Shepherd, Colin   (58), 59, 63
Shore, Andy   (82)
Silver City Comet   12, 127, 133, (134-135), 136, (137)
Simpson Desert   115, 123
Spencer Street Station, Melbourne   130
Sunraysia   127, 130, (131), (132), 133
Susan, the telephonist   15
Sydney, NSW   11, 12, 127, 136, 140

Tarcoola, SA   120
Taylor family   22, (23), (26)
Tea and Sugar   12, 98, (99), (100-101), (102), 103, 104, (105), (106), 107, 108, 110, 111, 127
Todd, Sir Charles   119
Todd River, NT   113, 123
Toowoomba, Qld   22, 27
Tropic of Capricorn   51

Vagg, Lloyd   42, 43
Vale, Graeme   (137)

Warrnambool, Vic   127, 129
Watson, SA   (104), (105), (106), 107, 108
Westlander   (34), 35, 36, 39, 42
Wheeler, Patrick   (58), 63
Willis, Bill   (102), 103, 104, 107, 108
Wroblewski, Janusz   76, 77, (77), 79, (82), 83
Wyndham, WA   70, 73

XPT   127, 133, 136, 140

Zanthus, WA   110